LET'S S⭐UND AMERICAN!

U.S. English Pronunciation Guide

Volume 2: Consonant Sounds

VICTOR GARCIA

VIC

COMPASS
PRESS

*To all my friends learning English
as a second language,
and my mom, my everything.*

Prologue

T he English language is well-known for its rich tapestry of sounds and phonetic rules that makes it an intricate path for individuals learning English as a second language. While you can memorize hundreds of words, master numerous grammatical rules and even speak fluently, what will give you that final polish to your continued and dedicated learning process is perfecting your pronunciation.

Be known that pronunciation refers to how you say each syllable of a word, while accent relates to the rhythm and melody of a language. An accent is linked to culture, therefore it is harder to modify. There's actually no need for you to do that! Directing your attention toward improving pronunciation will lead to more influential achievements while keeping yourself natural and proud of your origins.

When it comes to languages, the most important thing is conveying effective communication and making people understand what you say. However, every language has sounds that might not exist in others; which makes them unique yet challenging, when you try to reproduce those sounds with the ones you already know from your first language.

The foundation of enhancing your pronunciation is recognizing all of the sounds that legitimately are a mystery to you. Then you should learn rules that compartmentalize them and facilitate a better understanding. English is a wonderfully irregular language; so you will inevitably come across exemptions at a somewhat high extent, which can make rules seem questionable.

This is where this book especially offers a different approach by presenting you with an extensive array of examples for practicing pronunciation. At the same time, your vocabulary will benefit from exposure to the wide range of words, enabling you to look up their meanings and incorporate them into your lexicon.

In my personal journey as a fervent English learner, there were essential steps that helped me improve my pronunciation. The first and arguably most important is accurately learning the correct pronunciation of a phoneme from the beginning. Firstly, you should be able to hear the difference between every sound, even the most similar and confusing to you. Secondly, visualize how it is produced in the mouth with all the anatomical structures involved. And thirdly, practice and practice until you can replicate it with clarity and accuracy. Audio recording yourself and listening to it is provenly the best way to identify the imperfections.

Afterward, you should learn the spellings of each phoneme; read and audio record a large number of examples; compare it to the model recording and, most importantly, make corrections. It's crucial to go beyond single words; reading aloud tongue twisters, books or articles of any topic may have a substantial impact. This also applies to your daily speech when you mispronounce a word; you should always rectify it. Foremost, perform this exercise at least once a day on a regular basis; as with any skill, improvement comes through repetition and practice.

Being immersed in the language environment will undeniably accelerate the progress since the frequency of practice is essential to developing a foundation of long-term muscle memory. Practicing with both active and passive interaction helps to develop muscle memory and fluency. In the course of time, it helps learners to speak with a neutral cadence and rhythm.

Do not forget to run at your own pace. Self-awareness of your learning skills and cultivating patience come to play a pivotal role in your motivation and enthusiasm. Ultimately, these internal factors shape your path toward sustained progress and proficiency.

May this be just the beginning of a thrilling and rewarding journey toward your ultimate goal!

Introduction

A phoneme is the smallest unit of sound in a word; it can be a sound like /æ/ or /m/ or a group of different sounds like /oʊ/ or /aɪ/. The word *"sit"* is composed of three phonemes or sounds: /s/, /ɪ/, /t/. To identify phonemes, speak the word out loud. Listen to each separate sound.

Since the number of phonemes or speech sounds in English is greater than the number of letters in the alphabet (5 vowels and 21 consonants), a single sound could have multiple letter combinations. Notice that not every letter in a written word is a phoneme; some letters work together to form a single sound like *"ough"* in *"through"* to form /uː/. English orthography is not as strongly phonemic as that of many other languages.

The number and distribution of phonemes in English vary from dialect to dialect, and also depend on the interpretation of the individual researcher. This book encompasses a total of 16 vowel sounds, 22 consonant sounds and 2 semivowels. It is primarily focused on General American English, but acknowledges 4 other vowel sounds from British English, also known as Received Pronunciation.

Linguists have assigned a unique and unambiguous symbol to transcribe the speech sounds from all known spoken languages, creating the International Phonetic Alphabet (IPA). English uses just a limited subset of all the attested phonemes.

monophthongs				diphthongs			
iː sheep	**ɪ** ship	**ʊ** look	**uː** food	**ɪə** zero	**eɪ** basic		
ɛ red	**ə** about	**ɜː** bird	**ɔː** corn	**ʊə** jury	**ɔɪ** boy	**oʊ** go	
æ cat	**ʌ** cut	**ɑː** car	**ɒ** lock	**eə** area	**aɪ** kind	**aʊ** out	
p put	**b** boat	**t** time	**d** day	**tʃ** chair	**dʒ** job	**k** king	**g** get
f feel	**v** very	**θ** thing	**ð** there	**s** see	**z** zoo	**ʃ** ship	**ʒ** usual
m more	**n** new	**ŋ** song	**h** how	**l** life	**r** right	**w** warm	**j** year

VOWELS / CONSONANTS

☐ long ☐ short ☐ voiced ☐ unvoiced

The vowel sounds can be split into monophthongs and diphthongs. Within monophthongs you may find short and long vowels. Short vowels are: /ɪ/ - p*i*t, /ɛ/ - p*e*t, /æ/ - p*a*t, /ʌ/ - c*u*t, /ʊ/ - p*u*t, /ə/ - *a*bout. British English also presents /ɒ/ - d*o*g. Long vowels are: /iː/ - n*ee*d, /ɑː/ - h*a*rd, /ɔː/ - l*o*rd, /ɜː/ - p*ea*rl, /uː/ - f*oo*d. The triangular colon /ː/ indicates a vowel that is longer than others. All these monophthongs are a single vowel sound within a syllable; they are considered pure vowel sounds.

On the other hand, diphthongs contain two different vowel sounds in one syllable. They are sometimes called *"gliding vowels"* as the pronunciation of one vowel sound *"glides"* to another. There are 5 diphthongs: /eɪ/ - b*a*sic, /aɪ/ - *i*con, /ɔɪ/ - c*oi*n, /oʊ/ - g*o*, /aʊ/ - *ou*t. In British English, there are other three: /ɪə/ - h*e*ro, /eə/ - c*are*, /ʊə/ - s*ure*.

While vowels correspond to the most sonorous part of the syllable, consonants, in contrast, are the less sonorous margins. They are articulated with complete or partial closure of the vocal tract. There are also semivowels or semiconsonants.

Consonants are divided into unvoiced or voiceless and voiced. An unvoiced-voiced consonant pair consists of two consonant sounds, one an unvoiced sound, the other a voiced sound, with near-identical place and manner of articulation. These are the 8 consonant pairs: /p/ - /b/, /t/ - /d/, /k/ - /g/, /f/ - /v/, /θ/ - /ð/, /s/ - /z/, /ʃ/ - /ʒ/, /tʃ/ - /dʒ/.

Unvoiced consonant means that there is no vibration or voice coming from the voicebox when the sound is pronounced. The unvoiced consonants are: /p/ - _pill_, /t/ - _teach_, /k/ - _color_, /f/ - _flower_, /θ/ - _think_, /s/ - _simple_, /ʃ/ - _shame_, /tʃ/ - _chase_, /h/ - _heat_.

Otherwise, voiced consonant means that there is voice or vibration coming from the voicebox when the sound is pronounced. Within voiced consonants you can find: /b/ - _blue_, /d/ - _dance_, /g/ - _game_, /v/ - _vast_, /ð/ - _though_, /z/ - _zoo_, /ʒ/ - _genre_, /dʒ/ - _job_, /l/ - _lake_, /r/ - _red_, /m/ - _magic_, /n/ - _night_, /ŋ/ - _spring_.

Semivowels or semiconsonants, also known as _"glides"_, are phonetically similar to vowels, but they function as the syllable boundary, rather than as the nucleus of a syllable. In addition, they are usually shorter than vowels. Semivowels are: /j/ - _year_, /w/ - _water_. /j/ and /w/ are near to the vowels _"ee"_ and _"oo"_ in _"seen"_ and _"moon"_, written /iː/ and /uː/ respectively.

Without a doubt, it is beneficial to understand the structures involved in the articulation of words. The image below may assist with this purpose.

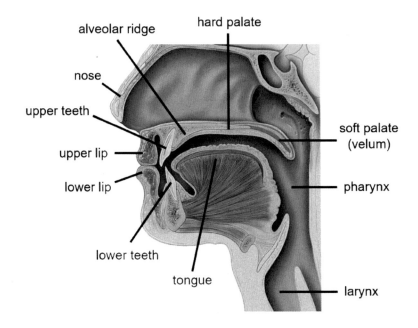

The articulators refer to any vocal organs involved in speech sound production. These organs can be categorized into two types: active or mobile ones, such as the tongue and lips, and passive or immobile ones, like the teeth, hard palate, etc.

The following is a chart of English consonants. There is some simplification, for example, all types of labials: bilabials /p/ /b/ /m/, labiodentals /f/ /v/ and the labiovelar /w/ are merged in the same column. Same with palatals: palato-alveolars /ʃ/ /ʒ/ /tʃ/ /dʒ/ /r/ and the palatal /j/.

In terms of manner of articulation, consonant sounds can be divided into obstruent and sonorant. An obstruent is formed by obstructing airflow. They contrast with sonorants, which do not

		Labial	Coronal			Back	
			Dental	Alveolar	Palatal	Velar	Glottal
Obstruent	Plosive	/p/ /b/		/t/ /d/		/k/ /g/	
	Fricative	/f/ /v/	/θ/ /ð/	/s/ /z/	/ʃ/ /ʒ/		/h/
	Affricate				/tʃ/ /dʒ/		
Sonorant	Nasal	/m/		/n/		/ŋ/	
	Approximant	/w/		/l/	/r/ /j/		

stop or cause turbulence in the airflow and resonate as a result. All obstruents are consonants, but sonorants include vowels as well as certain consonants. Whereas obstruents are frequently voiceless, sonorants are almost always voiced.

Obstruents are subdivided into plosives, fricatives and affricates. Plosives have complete occlusion of the vocal tract, often followed by a release burst. In contrast, fricatives have limited closure, not stopping airflow but making it turbulent. Fricatives of higher amplitude and pitch are called sibilants, which are made by directing a stream of air with the tongue toward the teeth. Lastly, affricates begin with complete occlusion but then transition into a fricative-like release.

On the other hand, sonorants, also called resonants, are divided into nasal consonants and approximants. Nasals allow air to escape through the nose but not through the mouth. Approximants are produced by bringing one articulator (tongue or lips) close to another without actually touching it; and they encompass the liquid consonants /l/ and /r/, and semivowels /j/ and /w/. In liquids, the tongue produces a partial closure in the mouth, without friction in roughly the same manner as a vowel.

The place of articulation is the point of contact where an obstruction occurs in the vocal tract between the tongue and another structure during the production of consonant sounds. It can be labial, dental, alveolar, palatal, velar, glottal, etcetera.

In phonetic notation, the mark /'/ above the line and before a syllable denotes that the syllable carries the principal accent or stress, as in *"hunter"* - /'hʌntər/. Conversely, the corresponding mark /ˌ/ below the line and before a syllable denotes that the syllable is accented slightly less than the primary one, as seen in *"shoemaker"* - /'ʃuˌmeɪkər/.

Every multisyllable word has a single stressed syllable. The main beat is placed on this one, carrying the most emphasis within the word. The remainder of syllables may have a secondary stress or be unstressed. While the stressed one is always said with a pure, unreduced vowel sound, the unstressed syllables use the reduced vowels schwa and /ɪ/, regardless of the spelling.

One curious aspect of accentuation is the contrast between noun-verb stress. The noun form typically has the stress on the first syllable, whereas the verb form has it on the second. For example, the word *"present"* as a noun is said /'prɛzənt/ and as a verb, /prɪ'zɛnt/. Other examples: *"record"* - /'rɛkərd/ (noun) and /rɪ'kɔːrd/ (verb); *"object"* - /'ɑːb.dʒɪkt/ (noun) and /əb'dʒɛkt/ (verb).

Furthermore, a noted difficulty of English is the high number of silent letters; they make the spelling of words different from their pronunciation. A letter is silent if it is not articulated; it does not correspond to any sound in the word's pronunciation. It may be an auxiliary letter that works with another to form a new sound.

Due to its widespread use in the English language, the magic "e" warrants its individual recognition. This phonetic marker indicates that the letter "e" at the end of a word doesn't produce a sound, but rather signals that a short vowel sound should generally be shifted into a long vowel sound. This "e" is the second letter in a split digraph with another vowel sound as seen in "da_te_". This digraph is interrupted by a consonant letter in the middle.

Another interesting aspect of English is the homophones, which are words that are pronounced exactly or nearly the same as another word but differ in meaning and are spelled differently. They are considered the most confusing words in the language.

In contrast, heteronyms are words that have a different pronunciation and meaning from another word but the same spelling. Additionally, minimal pairs are word pairs that differ by only one sound, which is normally confusing for English learners.

In this volume, your attention will be focused on the 22 consonants and the 2 semivowel sounds. Detailed information and diagrams will be provided for each sound, all their possible spellings and multiple examples of words for each spelling. As well as homophones and numerous minimal pairs for the big majority of these phonemes; along with a chapter dedicated to silent letters for the consonants in the English alphabet.

Every chapter exclusively highlights the spelling of the sound being discussed; therefore, it is advised to look up the full pronunciation of each word for accuracy. Keep in mind that these words reappear in other chapters with a different sound emphasized.

The e-book version includes hyperlinks to audiovisual content demonstrating the various phonetic sounds; in addition to several word examples illustrating the application of such sounds.

Disclaimer: This book contains curse words utilized strictly for educational purposes. The inclusion of such language is critical for the instructional goals of the material. Reader discretion is advised.

CONTENTS

Chapter 1

S

as in ***see***

T his phoneme represents the initial consonant sound in words such as *"sea"* and *"cell"*, as well as the final one in *"kiss"* and *"place"*. It is known for its distinctive high-pitched, easily detectable hissing sound. Therefore, it is commonly utilized to attract someone's attention with a call often written as *"sssst!"* or *"psssst!"* Its voiced counterpart is /z/.

This sound is described as an unvoiced alveolar sibilant fricative. The tip or blade of the tongue is placed against the alveolar ridge just behind the teeth. You direct the airstream along the center of the tongue and allow it to escape through the mouth only. It is produced without vibrations of the vocal cords.

The "s" at the beginning of words is always pronounced /s/.

sad, safe, sale, salt, same, sample, sand, save, say, sea,

> search, seat, second, see, sell, send, sense, service,
> set, several, side, sign, simple, since, sing, single, sink,
> sit, soap, soccer, social, some, song, soon, sort, sound,
> soup, success, suggest, suit, sun, suppose, surgeon,
> swan, swap, sweet, swift, swim, sword, symbol, system

By the same token, the initial "s" can also appear as a consonant cluster. Certain learners, particularly Spanish speakers, are advised to refrain from adding an /ə/ sound before /s/.

> scale, scar, schedule, scheme, school, screen, skate,
> ski, sky, sphere, slang, slate, slave, sleep, sleeve, slice,
> slide, slogan, slow, small, smart, smash, smell, smile,
> smirk, smith, smoke, snack, snake, snap, snatch, sneak,
> sneeze, snow, space, spare, spark, speak, speed, spell,
> spend, spin, spirit, spit, split, spoon, sport, spot, splash,
> spray, spread, spring, squad, squash, square, squat,
> squeeze, squid, staff, stage, stand, star, start, stay, step,
> still, stir, stone, stop, story, street, strong, study, style

Additionally, there are many words in which "s" is said as /s/ between vowels where it would be pronounced as /z/ in most other languages.

> aside, asylum, awesome, basic, basin, besides, bison,
> carousel, coliseum, comparison, diapason, dosage, epi-
> sode, gasoline, isolate, isosceles, isotope, leasing, mas-
> ochistic, mason, nuisance, obesity, parasite, philosophy,
> sausage, usage, venison

The following suffixes also feature this sound.

> abusive, derisive, divisive, explosive, invasive, curiosi-
> ty, nervosity, sinuosity, viscosity, analysis, basis, crisis,
> diagnosis, thesis, analyses, bases, crises, diagnoses,
> theses, courtesy, ecstasy, fantasy, hypocrisy, jealousy,
> leprosy, pleurisy

Similarly, when prefixes cause an "s" to be in the middle of a word, this "s" evokes /s/. Some examples: "sub-" and "mis-".

> subsist, subsequent, substantial, substandard, misun-
> derstand, mischief, misdemeanor, misread, mistake

This also occurs when the prefixes "de-", "dis-", "pre-" and "re-" have any stress.

> desalt, desexualize, disable, disappoint, disapprove, dis-
> order, dislike, preset, presell, presoak, resale, reset, re-
> seat, reseal, research, resell, resupply

As a result of assimilation, an "s" that is written next to an un-voiced consonant is almost always an unvoiced /s/.

> ask, risk, describe, discover, discuss, landscape, as-
> phalt, atmosphere, grasp, lisp, rasp, wasp, aspect, hos-
> pital, respect, response, assist, best, just, history, lob-
> ster, paste, system, trust, question, digestion, aesthetic,
> anesthesia

Curiously, when the unvoiced consonant is "t", the /t/ is silent if the next syllable is syllabic /l/ or /n/, otherwise it is pronounced.

> apostle, bristle, bustle, castle, hustle, nestle, pestle, rustle, thistle, whistle, wrestle, fasten, chasten, glisten, listen, moisten

However, there are certain examples with "s" said as /s/ next to a voiced consonant.

> /l/ - also, balsam, Nelson, convulsive, impulsive, repulsive
>
> /n/ - compensate, consent, consequence, consider, consist, consolation, consume, counsel, counselor, hansel, insist, ransom, responsible, sensitive, tinsel, expensive, extensive, pensive, constant, instead, transport
>
> /r/ - arson, conversation, morsel, persist, person, persuade, universal, university, versatile, versus, cursive, immersive, subversive, first, perspective
>
> absent, absolute, obsess, disdain, disgrace, disguise, disgusting

On the other hand, you can find the /s/ at the end of words.

> us, this, its, it's, yes, thus, gas, bus, plus, pus, alias, atlas, bias, canvas, Christmas, chaos, cosmos, axis, iris,

pelvis, penis, tennis, analysis, basis, crisis, diagnosis, parenthesis, thesis, appendicitis, arthritis, gastritis, hepatitis, chorus, circus, focus, genius, versus, famous, previous, hideous, continuous, perhaps, politics

In the same way, the final "s" in plural nouns, verbs in the third-person singular and Saxon genitive assimilates to the final voiceless consonant sound and is pronounced as /s/.

/p/ - *cups, drops, shops, sleeps, stops, ship's, Phillip's*

/t/ - *hats, lots, students, gets, hits, sits, writes, Robert's*

/k/ - *books, cooks, drinks, looks, talks, walks, Denmark's*

/f/ - *beliefs, chiefs, cliffs, roofs, laughs, sniffs, Jeff's*

/θ/ - *cloths, months, myths, paths, truths, Ruth's*

In addition, you can find the /s/ at the end of words using the magic "e". The "s" is usually preceded by the sounds below.

Vowels - *base, case, chase, blouse, mouse, dose, glucose, morose, goose, loose, moose, masseuse, cease, grease, increase, lease, release, obese, siamese, concise, paradise, precise, anise, promise, purchase, purpose, porpoise, tortoise*

/l/ - *else, false, pulse, convulse, expulse, impulse*

/r/ - coar**se**, cour**se**, cur**se**, conver**se**, diver**se**, hor**se**, immer**se**, mor**se**, nur**se**, rehear**se**, remor**se**, ver**se**, uni-ver**se**, wor**se**

/n/ - den**se**, expen**se**, inten**se**, licen**se**, respon**se**, rin**se**, sen**se**, ten**se**

/p/ - apocaly**pse**, colla**pse**, cor**pse**, ecli**pse**, ela**pse**, el-li**pse**, glim**pse**, la**pse**, prola**pse**, syna**pse**

Moreover, the following words feature the /s/ when used as nouns or adjectives.

abu**se**, clo**se**, diffu**se**, excu**se**, hou**se**, u**se**

There are some words that present a silent "s" in their spelling.

i**s**land, i**s**le, ai**s**le, vi**s**count, debri**s**, chassi**s**, preci**s**, bour-geoi**s**, patoi**s**, travoi**s**, rendezvou**s**, **s**chwa, Arkansa**s**

Conversely, the letter "s" is sometimes accompanied by a silent letter and both together are pronounced as /s/.

Silent "w" - an**sw**er, **sw**ord

Silent "th" - i**sth**mus

Silent "p" - **ps**alm, **ps**eudo, **ps**eudonym, **ps**oriasis, **ps**ych, **ps**ychic, **ps**ychology, **ps**ychiatry, **ps**ychiatrist, **ps**ycho-therapy, **ps**ychedelic, **ps**ychopath, **ps**ychotic

6

The *"ss"* most often forms the /s/ sound, whether it occurs in the middle or at the end of words.

Middle Position - *assess, assign, assist, associate, assume, accessible, admissible, bassinet, classism, colossal, croissant, essential, fossil, glossary, gossip, lesson, massage, masseuse, message, missile, necessary, odyssey, passage, possible, vessel, aggressive, massive, missive*

Final Position - *access, accross, address, assess, boss, class, cross, discuss, dress, glass, kiss, less, loss, mass, mattress, miss, pass, press, process, stress, business, darkness, illness*

Magic *"e"* - *bagasse, impasse, mousse, finesse, noblesse, lacrosse*

Peculiarly, it can occasionally be pronounced as two /s/, represented as /s.s/.

disservice, dyssomnia, misspeak, misspell, missell, disseat, missort

Another spelling for /s/ is the letter *"c"* + magic *"e"*.

chance, dance, nuance, peace, piece, niece, police, prince, since, divorce, force, source, sauce, introduce, juice, produce, reduce, fence, hence, once, advice, ice, nice, price, sacrifice, twice, ace, face, grace, place, race, space, trace, choice, voice, absence, balance, conference, distance, evidence, experience, instance, nuisance, penance, science, sentence, silence, violence, jaundice, justice, notice, office, palace, practice, prejudice, service, surface. The "ce" is silent in "Worcester", "Leicester" and other U.K. cities ending in "-cester".

Nevertheless, the letter "c" represents /s/ before the letters "e", "i" and "y". This sound is known as the soft "c".

"e" - ceiling, celebrate, cell, cellar, cellophane, cent, center, central, century, certain, cancel, chancellor, concern, December, decent, procedure, process, receive, reception, recent

"i" - cigarette, Cinderella, cinema, circle, circumstance, citizen, city, civil, associate, association, capacity, council, criticism, decide, decision, decimal, electricity, enunciate, enunciation, exercise, incident, precise, principal, principle, pronunciate, pronunciation, society, solicit, specific

"y" - cyan, cyber, cyborg, cycle, cynical, cypher, cyst, agency, fancy, currency, democracy, efficiency, emergency, icy, juicy, Lucy, mercy, policy, privacy, racy, spicy

You can oddly find the word below presenting a letter "c" as /s/ despite being followed by an "a".

facade

Additionally, the *"sc"* spelling followed by *"e"*, *"i"* and *"y"* evokes /s/ in all these words.

> *"e"* - s**c**enario, s**c**enery, s**c**ene, s**c**ent, abs**c**end, abs**c**ess, adoles**c**ent, as**c**end, cres**c**ent, des**c**end, fluores**c**ent, obs**c**ene. Examples with magic *"e"*: evanes**c**e, reminis**c**e.

> *"i"* - s**c**ience, s**c**ientific, s**c**ientist, s**c**issors, dis**c**iple, dis-**c**ipline, fas**c**inate, resus**c**itate

> *"y"* - s**c**ythe

The word below is one of the few exceptions of the previous rule, in which *"sc"* is followed by *"l"*.

> *mus**c**le*

On the other hand, the double *"c"* before *"e"* or *"i"* should be pronounced as /ks/.

> *"e"* - a**cc**elerate, a**cc**ent, a**cc**ept, a**cc**ess, a**cc**essory, e**c**-**c**entric, su**cc**ess

> *"i"* - a**cc**ident, fla**cc**id, o**cc**ident, o**cc**ipital, va**cc**ine

By the same token, the letter *"x"* most often forms a blend of two unvoiced consonant sounds: /k/ and /s/. *"x"* always mani-fests this /ks/ when it appears at the end of the word.

> *bo**x**, fa**x**, fi**x**, fo**x**, fle**x**, hoa**x**, mi**x**, o**x**, po**x**, se**x**, si**x**, ta**x**,*

> *affix, apex, complex, equinox, index, latex, matrix, relax, jinx, lynx, minx, larynx, pharynx*

Same occurs when the "x" is followed by a voiceless consonant.

> *excavation, exchange, exclusive, excuse, Oxford, exhale, expand, expect, expensive, experience, expert, explain, explore, export, express, exquisite, next, text, context, extend, extinguish, extra, mixture, ambidextrous*

Whereas, "x" within vowel sounds features the /ks/ when the "x" is preceded by a stressed syllable.

> *approximate, axel, boxer, execute, exercise, exhibition, exigent, flexible, galaxy, hexagon, maximum, Mexico, oxide, oxygen, pixel, proxy, saxophone, sexy, taxi, Texas, toxic, tuxedo*

The digraph "xc" always utilizes /ks/ as well.

> *exceed, excel, excellent, except, excess, excise, excite*

In a special manner, these two words can use either /ks/ or /gz/.

> *exit, exile*

And the digraphs "zz" and "tz" produce the pattern /ts/.

> *mezzo, mozzarella, paparazzi, pizza, pretzel, ritzy, quartz, ritz, waltz*

Lastly, the following homophones contain the sound /s/.

cent - scent - sent   sale - sail

it's - its   sea - see - C

mist - missed   some - sum

past - passed   son - sun

It is beneficial to know about the phonological process known as voicing or sonorization; in which a normally voiceless consonant becomes voiced when adjacent to voiced sounds. This may occur at the beginning if preceded by a voiced sound or at the end if followed by a voiced sound. It commonly happens when speaking fast. The words listed below could exhibit this phenomenon; with the voiceless /s/ sound being voiced to /z/.

better sleep, broad smile, circus benches, false gesture, famous doctor, lobster, loose gown, mainstream, precise numbers, previous name, purchase them, release them, small snack, sunscreen, this job, this moment, this voice

Please, don't forget to record yourself saying the words, compare it to the model and make any necessary corrections. It is advisable to repeat this exercise on a daily basis. Furthermore, consider writing and practicing with tongue twisters and sentences that emphasize the pronunciation of /s/ in various topics and daily life scenarios.

Chapter 2

Z

as in <u>z</u>oo

This phoneme represents the initial consonant sound in words such as *"<u>z</u>one"* and *"<u>z</u>oo"* and the final one in *"pri<u>ze</u>"* and *"ja<u>zz</u>"*, as well as, the *"s"* as in *"wa<u>s</u>"* or *"ea<u>sy</u>"*. It has a characteristic hissing effect. Its unvoiced counterpart is /s/.

This sound is described as a voiced alveolar sibilant fricative. The tip or blade of the tongue is placed at the alveolar ridge just behind the teeth. You direct the airstream along the center of the tongue and allow it to escape through the mouth only, causing high-frequency turbulence. Vibrate your vocal cords as you make this sound.

An *"s"* that is written between two vowels is usually /z/. See the following examples sorted by the vowel following *"s"*.

"a" - *accusation, advisable, appraisal, arousal, artisan,*

causal, cesarean, disaster, disposable, disposal, mosaic, nasal, partisan, peasant, pheasant, pleasant, proposal, prosaic, refusal, reprisal, rosary, thousand, visa

"e" - closet, diesel, disease, eraser, fuselage, geyser, Joseph, laser, measles, miserable, misery, museum, poseur, represent, rosette, teaser, trousers, user, weasel

"i" - acquisition, amusing, aphrodisiac, basil, bourgeoisie, composition, cousin, cuisine, deposit, desirable, divisible, easily, enthusiasm, enthusiastic, exquisite, feasible, gymnasium, hesitate, invisible, limousine, music, opposite, opposition, physical, physiological, physician, plausible, position, positive, president, proposition, raisin, requisite, risible, visible, visit

"o" - advisory, bosom, divisor, incisor, liaison, mausoleum, poison, prison, prisoner, reason, season, treason

"u" - usurp

"y" - busy, cheesy, daisy, drowsy, easy, lousy, noisy, nosy, posy, queasy, rosy

When prefixes "de-", "pre-" and "re-" are unstressed, the following "s" is pronounced as /z/ if the "s" comes before a vowel.

deserve, desert, design, desire, desist, presence, present, preserve, preside, presume, presuntive, resemble, *resent, reserve, reservoir, reside, resident, residue, re-sidual, resign, resilience, resilient, resin, resist, resistant, resolve, resolution, resort, resound, resonance, reso-nant, resume, result, resurrect*

Additionally, an "s" that is written next to a voiced consonant and assimilates to the consonant, is always voiced /z/.

/b/ - husband, lesbian, absorb, absorption, absurd, ob-serve

/d/ - wisdom, Tuesday, Wednesday, Thursday, poised

/g/ - disgrace, disguise, disgusting

/m/ - abysmal, bridesmaid, charisma, cosmetic, cosmo-politan, cosmos, dismal, embourgeoisement, jasmin, mesmerize, seismic, crimson, clumsy, damsel, flimsy, whimsical, whimsy

palsy, berserk, Jersey, kersey, business, transaction, transit, transition, transsexual, forensic, intrinsic, Kan-sas, pansy, quinsy, tansy, teensy

By the same token, an "s" is always voiced /z/ when the letter combination "-sm" appears at the end of a word, in which case a reduced vowel sound /ə/ is produced between "s" and "m".

chasm, prism, plasm, spasm, activism, altruism, athe-

> *ism, autism, baptism, capitalism, criticism, exorcism, heroism, humanism, journalism, masochism, material-ism, mechanism, metabolism, nationalism, nepotism, optimism, organism, orgasm, phantasm, racism, real-ism, sarcasm, sexism, terrorism, tourism*

In a few words, the letter "s" + a silent letter are adjacent to a voiced consonant, manifesting the /z/.

> *asthma, Christmas, raspberry, corps*

On the other hand, you can find the /z/ spelled as "s" at the end of words.

> *as, does, has, his, hers, is, was, theirs, always, besides, sometimes, diabetes, herpes, isosceles, gallows, lens, measles, news, series, species, newspaper*

Words of Greek origin ending in "-sis" /sɪs/ make their plurals ending in "-ses" /siːz/.

> *analyses, bases, crises, diagnoses, doses, theses*

Similarly, the final "s" in plural nouns, verbs in the third-person singular and Saxon genitive assimilates to the final voiced consonant sound and is pronounced as /z/.

> /b/ - *crabs, cribs, jobs, verbs, grabs, rubs, scrubs, sobs, Bob's, Caleb's*

/d/ - be**ds**, car**ds**, frien**ds**, wor**ds**, decide**s**, en**ds**, fin**ds**, ri**des**, Edwar**d's**, Finlan**d's**

/g/ - ba**gs**, do**gs**, dru**gs**, eg**gs**, be**gs**, di**gs**, dra**gs**, hu**gs**, Crai**g's**

/v/ - glov**es**, nerv**es**, slav**es**, arriv**es**, driv**es**, Dave**'s**. Some nouns ending in "-f" and "-fe" change their spelling to "-ves" when becoming plural: *calf - cal**ves**, half - hal**ves**, knife - kni**ves**, life - li**ves**, loaf - loa**ves**, shelf - shel**ves**, thief - thie**ves**.*

/ð/ - cloth**es**, bath**es**, breath**es**. Some nouns ending in "-th" change their pronunciation from /θ/ to /ðz/: *bath - bath**s**, booth - booth**s**, mouth - mouth**s**, oath - oath**s**, path - path**s**, truth - truth**s**, youth - youth**s**, wreath - wreath**s**.*

/l/ - hospital**s**, hotel**s**, school**s**, wheel**s**, deal**s**, fail**s**, feel**s**, fill**s**, Caro**l's**, Danie**l's**

/r/ - barbe**rs**, ca**rs**, guita**rs**, leade**rs**, sho**res**, ente**rs**, fea**rs**, hea**rs**, pou**rs**, sha**res**, Esthe**r's**, Jennife**r's**

/m/ - album**s**, dream**s**, poem**s**, problem**s**, room**s**, claim**s**, form**s**, inform**s**, scream**s**, seem**s**, Willia**m's**, Graha**m's**

/n/ - coi**ns**, garde**ns**, pla**ns**, thor**ns**, weapo**ns**, imagi**nes**, joi**ns**, maintai**ns**, remai**ns**, tur**ns**, Calvi**n's**, Londo**n's**

/ŋ/ - *earrings, kings, things, tongues, belongs, brings, rings, sings, Stirling's*

Since all vowel sounds are voiced, you also use /z/ when the word ends in a vowel sound, including the *"-es"* after *"o"*, and *"y"* preceded by a consonant. If you make a contraction of words like *"she is"* and create *"she's"*, that *"s"* is pronounced as /z/.

dominoes, echoes, heroes, potatoes, photos, zeros, bodies, keys, toys, shoes, goes, blows, vows, marries, worries, sees, plays, stays, cries, fries, lies, enjoys, chews, Mary's, she's, he's

Otherwise, plural nouns, verbs in the third-person singular and Saxon genitive of words ending in fricative and affricate sounds are made by creating another syllable, the *"-es"* ending, which is pronounced as /ɪz/ or /əz/.

/s/ - *bosses, boxes, nurses, places, denounces, fixes, kisses, releases, rinses, Alice'(ə)s, Alex'(ə)s*

/z/ - *cruises, espouses, noses, prizes, roses, abuses, buzzes, erases, raises, rises, freezes, Cruz'(ə)s*

/ʃ/ - *dishes, washes, wishes, Dash'(ə)s*

/tʃ/ - *churches, couches, inches, matches, approaches, catches, fetches, switches, Aldrich'(ə)s*

/ʒ/ - *collages, garages, massages*

/ʤ/ - *ages, images, oranges, sausages, charges, changes, engages, merges, George'(ə)s*

In addition, if a word ends in "-se" preceded by a vowel, the "s" will often form the /z/ sound. The examples below are organized by vowel sound preceding the /z/.

/iː/ - *cheese, ease, please, tease, these, appease, chemise, disease, expertise, reprise, striptease, Chinese, Japanese*

/uː/ - *fuse, muse, ruse, accuse, amuse, confuse, defuse, enthuse, infuse, refuse, bruise, cruise, choose, lose, whose*

/ɔː/ - *cause, because, clause, pause, applause*

/oʊ/ - *those, hose, nose, pose, prose, rose, compose, diagnose, disclose, dispose, enclose, expose, impose, propose, oppose, repose, suppose*

/aʊ/ - *browse, arouse, carouse, espouse*

/eɪ/ - *braise, chaise, phase, phrase, praise, raise, vase, appraise, erase, liaise, malaise, mayonnaise*

/ɔɪ/ - *noise, poise, turquoise*

/ɛ/ - *cleanse*

The following words undergo a voicing or sonorization process, which changes the unvoiced /s/ of nouns to a voiced /z/, when forming their verb pairs.

> abuse, close, diffuse, excuse, house, use

In a similar fashion, the suffix "-ise" when it is used to form verbs will reliably produce the /z/ sound. In American English, these are much more commonly represented by "-ize" instead, but there are a few words that must be spelled "-ise".

> advertise, advise, arise, chastise, comprise, compromise, demise, despise, devise, disguise, enterprise, excise, exercise, franchise, guise, improvise, incise, revise, rise, sunrise, supervise, surmise, surprise, televise, wise, likewise, otherwise, clockwise

The "ss" can occasionally form the /z/ sound in certain words in which it appears between two vowels. There are only a few words in which this is the case.

> Aussie, brassiere, dessert, dissolve, hussar, Missouri, possess, possession, scissors

On the other hand, the "z" is always pronounced as /z/. It can be found in different positions within words. When at the end, it is usually (but not always) doubled.

> Initial Position - zag, zap, zeal, zealous, zebra, zig, zinc, zip, zero, zodiac, zone, zoo, zoom, zucchini

Middle Position - *cozy, crazy, hazy, lazy, Amazon, bazaar, bizarre, bulldozer, citizen, dozen, eczema, emblazon, enzyme, gazette, hazard, hazel, horizon, horizontal, influenza, lizard, magazine, marzipan, plaza, razor, tweezers, wizard, amazing, blazing, freezing, seizing*

Final Position - *quiz, topaz, buzz, fizz, jazz*

Magic "e" - *amaze, blaze, booze, breeze, bronze, daze, freeze, gauze, gaze, glaze, graze, haze, maize, maze, prize, raze, seize, size, squeeze*

The most common use of "z" is in the suffix "-ize" and its derivative "-ization". In British English, these suffixes are more commonly spelled "-ise" and "-isation".

"-ze" - *analyze, apologize, authorize, baptize, capitalize, categorize, characterize, civilize, colonize, criticize, customize, dialyze, emphasize, eulogize, fertilize, idealize, immunize, jeopardize, legalize, localize, maximize, mesmerize, minimize, memorize, neutralize, optimize, organize, polarize, realize, recognize, specialize, summarize, sympathize, synchronize, theorize, utilize, visualize, vocalize*

"-ization" - *authorization, civilization, colonization, dramatization, fertilization, generalization, optimization, organization, realization, specialization, sterilization, visualization*

Besides, some words present *"zz"* in a middle position.

> *blizzard, buzzard, dazzle, dizzy, fizzle, fuzzy, muzzle, nozzle, puzzle, tizzy*

Nevertheless, these following two words contain a silent *"z"*.

> *laissez-faire, rendezvous*

The *"x"* at the beginning of words normally spells /z/.

> *xanthan, Xavier, xenolith, xerography, xenon, xenophobia, xylophone*

In addition, when the *"x"* appears immediately before the stressed syllable of the word and it is followed by a vowel, it becomes voiced as the combination /gz/.

> *Alexander, auxiliary, exact, exactly, exaggerate, exalt, exaltation, exam, examine, examination, example, exasperate, executive, exempt, exert, exist, existence, existential, exotic, exuberant, exude*

This includes silent *"h"* in the middle of *"x"* and voiced consonant.

> *exhaust, exhibit, exhilarate, exhort, exhume*

These two words can be pronounced with either /ks/ or /gz/.

> *exit, exile*

Equivalently, the digraph *"nx"* in the following word is pronounced /ŋz/.

a**nx**iety

The homophones listed below contain the sound /z/.

clau**se** - claw**s**	si**ze** - sigh**s**	rai**se** - ray**s**
free**ze** - free**s**	pau**se** - paw**s**	way**s** - weigh**s**

It is also worth noting that *"plea<u>se</u>"* and *"lea<u>se</u>"* don't rhyme. Likewise, *"demi<u>se</u>"* and *"conci<u>se</u>"*, *"compromi<u>se</u>"* and *"promi<u>se</u>"*.

There are also a few heteronyms.

pre**s**ent - as /ˈprezənt/ means the current moment or gift
as /prɪˈzent/ means to reveal

u**se** - as /juːs/ means function or benefit
as /juːz/ means employ or utilize

u**se**d to - as /juːst tə/ is the modal verb
as /juːzd tə/ is the normal verb followed by *"to"*

Furthermore, you can find a curious contrast in the following words. The first word of the pair contains /s/ and the second, /z/.

abu**s**ive - abu**s**er	aby**ss** - aby**s**mal
a**ss**ess - po**ss**ess	divi**s**ive - divi**s**or

exhibition - exhibit   *crisis - crises*
louse - lousy   *thesis - theses*

Lastly, it is useful to know about the phonological process known as devoicing; in which a normally voiced consonant is replaced by a voiceless one when adjacent to unvoiced sounds. This may occur at the beginning if preceded by an unvoiced sound or at the end if followed by an unvoiced sound. It commonly happens when speaking fast. The words listed below often exhibit this phenomenon; with the voiced /z/ being devoiced to /s/.

> *suppose to, supposed to, has to, used to, newspaper, cheese cake, Chinese town, cruise ship, his father, his problem, lose track of time, refuse service, these flowers, whose pencil*

Please, don't forget to record yourself saying the words, compare it to the model and make any necessary corrections. It is advisable to repeat this exercise on a daily basis. Furthermore, consider writing and practicing with tongue twisters and sentences that emphasize the pronunciation of /z/ in various topics and daily life scenarios.

Chapter 3

Minimal Pairs

S *and* Z

T he phoneme /s/ is articulated with the tongue positioned further back in the mouth and with a wider opening. On the other hand, /z/ is a voiced counterpart of /s/, producing a smoother sound that can be prolonged as desired.

ace - A's	false - falls
advice - advise	grace - graze
bus - buzz	gross - grows
base - bays	hiss - his
cease - seas	ice - eyes - I's
close (adj.) - close (v.)	juice - Jews
dose - doughs	lacy - lazy
dice - dies	loose - lose
face - phase	loss - laws

niece - knees

once - ones

pace - pays

peace, piece - peas, P's

place - plays

precedent - president

price - prize

race - raise, rays

racer - razor

rice - rise

scarce - scares

since - sins

spice - spies

Sue - zoo

tense - tens

trace - trays

∫

as in **ship**

T his phoneme represents the initial consonant sound in words such as *"she"*, *"show"* and *"shop"*, and the final one in *"ash"*, *"cash"* and *"fish"*. Its voiced counterpart is /ʒ/.

This sound is described as an unvoiced palato-alveolar sibilant fricative. The blade of the tongue touches the roof of the mouth behind the alveolar ridge, while the front is arched upward toward the hard palate. You direct the airstream toward the center of the tongue and release it through the mouth only, creating high-frequency turbulence. It is produced without vibrations of the vocal cords.

The most common spelling for this sound is *"sh"*. Listed below you can find multiple examples with this spelling in different positions.

Initial Position - *shade, shadow, shaft, shake, shall, shallow, shame, shampoo, shape, share, sharp, shave, shaw, she, shear, shed, sheep, sheer, sheet, shelf, shell, shelter, shepherd, sheriff, shield, shift, shill, shimmer, shin, shine, ship, shire, shirt, shit, shiver, shock, shoe, shoot, shop, shore, short, shop, shot, should, shoulder, shout, shove, shovel, show, shower, shuck, shudder, shuffle, shun, shush, shutter, shuttle, shut, shy*

Middle Position - *bishop, eggshell, cushion, fashion, flashlight, hashbrown, lasher, relationship, sunshine, threshold*

Final Position - *accomplish, anguish, ash, blush, brush, bush, cash, clash, crash, crush, dash, diminish, dish, distinguish, establish, extinguish, fetish, finish, fish, flash, flesh, flush, foolish, fresh, furnish, harsh, leash, marsh, parish, polish, publish, punish, push, rash, relish, rush, selfish, shush, slash, smash, splash, squash, stash, stylish, trash, vanish, varnish, wash, wish*

In words of French origin, /ʃ/ can be spelled "ch". The following words exemplify the previously stated.

Initial Position - *chagrin, chaise, chalet, champagne, chandelier, chaperone, charade, charlatan, chasseur, chassis, chateau, chauffeur, chauvinist, chef, chemise, chenille, chic, chiffon, chivalry, chute, Charlotte, Chevrolet, Chicago*

Middle Position - *attaché, brochure, cachet, cliché, crochet, echelon, machete, machine, machinery, nonchalant, parachute, penchant, pistachio, ricochet, sachet, Michelle, Michigan*

Final Position - *cache, douche, gauche, louche, niche, quiche, ruche, gouache, mustache, panache, pastiche*

Additionally, the sound /ʃ/ can also be spelled with "s". The ending "-sion" preceded by the consonants "l" and "n" always uses /ʃ/. As well as the few words preceded by "r" that are listed below.

"l" - *convulsion, compulsion, expulsion, repulsion*

"n" - *dimension, expansion, extension, mansion, pension, suspension, tension*

"r" - *immersion, torsion, controversial*

In the same way, the letter "s" followed by "u" is pronounced as /ʃ/ in the next examples.

sugar, sure, censure, ensure, insurance, sensual, consensual, sensuous

The words below oddly contain this sound spelled as "s" followed by "e".

nauseous, Sean

By the same token, the suffix "-ssion" will always make the /ʃ/ sound. There are also a few words with "ss" followed by "i" that exhibit this phoneme.

> "ssion" - *admission, aggression, commission, confession, depression, discussion, expression, fission, impression, mission, obsession, passion, permission, possession, profession, progression, session, succession, transmission*
>
> *passional, professional, commissioner, passionate, Russia, Russian, hessian*

Furthermore, "ss" followed by "u" is also pronounced as /ʃ/ in the following words.

> *assure, fissure, pressure, scissure, issue, tissue*

On the other hand, the letter "c" represents /ʃ/ before the letters "e" and "i" in the examples below.

> "e" - *ocean, cetacean, crustacean, herbaceous, opiaceos, sebaceous, violaceous*
>
> "i" - *specie, glacier, artificial, commercial, crucial, facial, financial, glacial, judicial, official, provincial, racial, social, spacial, special, superficial, electrician, magician, musician, obstetrician, optician, pediatrician, phonetician, physician, politician, technician, appreciate, cru-*

> *ciate, depreciate, excruciate, appreciation, excruciating, ancient, coefficient, efficient, deficient, sufficient, efficiency, sufficiency, coercion, suspicion, delicious, ferocious, gracious, malicious, precious, precocious, spacious, suspicious, vicious*

It can also be found as "c" + magic "e" in the following word.

> *licorice*

In contrast, the "c" can be pronounced either /s/ or /ʃ/ in the words below.

> *associate, association*

The "sc" spelling followed by "e" and "i" evokes /ʃ/ in a few examples.

> *crescendo, fascia, fascism, conscience, conscious, omniscience, omniscient, luscious, prosciutto*

Similarly, the ending "-tion" and derivatives always manifests /ʃ/; unless preceded by the letter "s", in which case it is said /tʃ/.

> *action, addition, ambition, assumption, attention, collection, competition, condition, definition, direction, distribution, education, exception, exhibition, evaluation, fiction, function, fraction, generation, investigation, institution, isolation, junction, location, lotion, mention,*

> motion, nation, notion, operation, option, population, position, potion, proportion, ration, reputation, section, situation, solution, station, tradition, vacation, valuation, variation, additional, emotional, exceptional, functional, institutional, national, optional, rational, traditional, conditioner, practitioner, stationer, vacationer, ambitious, cautious, infectious, nutritious

In addition, the letter combinations *"tia"* and *"tie"* are pronounced with /ʃ/ in the following words. There is also an example with *"tio"*.

> *"tia"* - initiative, essential, initial, partial, potential, substantial, torrential, Dalmatian, dietitian, Egyptian, Haitian, Martian, differentiate, initiate, negotiate, potentiate, satiate, expatiate, licentiate, differentiation, initiation, negotiation, potentiation, satiation
>
> *"tie"* - patience, patient, quotient, sentient
>
> *"tio"* - ratio

You can come across a few words containing *"sch"* said as /ʃ/.

> **sch**wa, **sch**ist

Same occurs with the sequence *"chs"*.

> fu**chs**ia

Last but not least, the "x" is exceptionally pronounced as /kʃ/.

> *sexual, sexuality, bisexual, heterosexual, homosexual, anxious, noxious, obnoxious, complexion, crucifixion, flexion, reflexion*

It is beneficial to know about the phonological process known as voicing or sonorization; in which a normally voiceless consonant becomes voiced when adjacent to voiced sounds. This commonly happens when speaking fast. The words listed below could feature this phenomenon; with the voiceless /ʃ/ sound being voiced to /ʒ/.

> *dashboard, flash drive, flashlight, fresh bread, freshwater, harsh voice, punish them, push yourself, selfish guy, stylish nails, trash bag, washbasin*

Please, don't forget to record yourself saying the words, compare it to the model and make any necessary corrections. It is advisable to repeat this exercise on a daily basis. Furthermore, consider writing and practicing with tongue twisters and sentences that emphasize the pronunciation of /ʃ/ in various topics and daily life scenarios.

as in **ʒ** *usual*

Τhis phoneme represents the consonant sound in words such as *"usually"* and *"genre"*. There aren't indeed many words with this sound on its own. Just a few of English words start with the phoneme /ʒ/. These words often originate from French and are typically pronounced in a French way. Its unvoiced counterpart is /ʃ/.

This sound is described as a voiced palato-alveolar sibilant fricative. The blade of the tongue touches the roof of the mouth behind the alveolar ridge, while the front is arched upward toward the hard palate. You direct the airstream toward the center of the tongue and release it through the mouth only, creating high-frequency turbulence. The vocal cords vibrate during the process.

Let's start by practicing the words below, in which the ending *"-sion"* preceded by the consonant *"r"* is pronounced with /ʒ/.

> *version, aversion, conversion, diversion, inversion, per-version, reversion, subversion, emersion, dispersion, submersion, excursion, incursion*

The ending *"-sion"* is always said with /ʒ/ when it's preceded by a vowel.

> *abrasion, evasion, invasion, occasion, persuasion, per-vasion, adhesion, cohesion, lesion, collision, decision, division, revision, incision, precision, provision, vision, television, corrosion, erosion, explosion, implosion, al-lusion, fusion, conclusion, confusion, delusion, diffu-sion, exclusion, illusion, inclusion, infusion, intrusion, protrusion, seclusion*

In addition, the suffix *"-sia"* is pronounced as /ʒ/. It is commonly utilized for denoting the names of medical conditions, regions or nations, or specific qualities or states.

> *ambrosia, amnesia, analgesia, anesthesia, aphasia, atresia, dysplasia, euthanasia, fantasia, kinesthesia, magnesia, Asia*

The ending *"-sual"* also manifests /ʒ/. It is found in only three adjectives, however these words can be further extended by adding other suffixes.

> *casual, casually, casualty, usual, usually, visual, visually, visuality*

Besides, the suffix "*-sure*" is said /ʒ/ when it is preceded by the letter "*o*", "*ea*" or "*ei*".

> clo**s**ure, compo**s**ure, disclo**s**ure, expo**s**ure, mea**s**ure, plea**s**ure, trea**s**ure, lei**s**ure

A few other words containing "*s*" as /ʒ/ include the following.

> ho**s**ier, nau**s**ea, parme**s**an

Curiously, there are two other words ending in "*-ure*" that create the /ʒ/, but they are spelled with a "*z*" rather than an "*s*".

> sei**z**ure, a**z**ure. The word "**zhuzh**" is a special case.

Furthermore, you can come across another word with a "*z*" spelling said as /ʒ/.

> bra**z**ier

The following loanwords from French contain /ʒ/ spelled as "*g*".

> Initial Position - **g**enre, **g**endarme
>
> Middle Position - auber**g**ine, bou**g**ie, embour**g**eoisement, bour**g**eois, lin**g**erie, re**g**ime
>
> Final Position - bei**g**e, rou**g**e, arbitra**g**e, barra**g**e, camoufla**g**e, colla**g**e, concier**g**e, corsa**g**e, dressa**g**e, entou-

> *rage, espionage, fuselage, garage, massage, melange,*
> *mirage, montage, sabotage*

On the other hand, it is also found with the spelling *"j"* in some other loanwords.

> *bijou, déjà vu, Beijing, jongleur, force-majeure, Taj Mahal*

You can oddly find this sound spelled as *"t"* in the word below.

> *equation*

Lastly, the *"x"* forms the /gʒ/ combination in these words.

> *luxury, luxurious*

It is useful to know about the phonological process known as devoicing; in which a normally voiced consonant is replaced by a voiceless one when adjacent to unvoiced sounds. This commonly happens when speaking fast. The words listed below could exhibit this phenomenon; with the voiced /ʒ/ being devoiced to /ʃ/.

> *beige color, collage techniques, garage parking, massage therapy*

Please, don't forget to record yourself saying the words, compare it to the model and make any necessary corrections. It is advisable to repeat this exercise on a daily basis.

/ʒ/

Furthermore, consider writing and practicing with tongue twisters and sentences that emphasize the pronunciation of /ʒ/ in various topics and daily life scenarios.

Chapter 6

Minimal Pairs

S *and* ʃ

The phoneme /ʃ/ is articulated with a much more rounded mouth as compared to the phoneme /s/. It is commonly used to signal for silence: *"Shhh! Be quiet!"* The phoneme /s/ is articulated with the lips retracted further than /z/, maintaining the same oral posture but without phonating.

ass - ash	gas - gash	said - shed
bass - bash	mass - mash	sail - shale
boss - bosh	mess - mesh	sake - shake
C - she	moss - mosh	sale - shale
cost - coshed	plus - plush	same - shame
crass - crash	puss - push	sank - shank
crust - crushed	rust - rushed	sass - sash
doss - dosh	sack - shack	save - shave
fist - fished	sag - shag	scene - sheen

sea - she	sin - shin
seal - she'll	sine - shine
seat - sheet	single - shingle
see - she	sip - ship
seed - she'd	sit - shit
seek - chic	so - show
seen - sheen	sock - shock
seer - sheer	son - shun
seize - she's	sore - sure
sell - shell	sort - short
sew - show	sucks - shucks
sift - shift	sue - shoe
sigh - shy	sun - shun
sign - shine	

tʃ

as in **chair**

This phoneme represents the initial consonant sound in words such as *"chain"* and *"choose"*, and the final one in *"each"* and *"catch"*. It can be explained as a short /t/ sound right before and merged with /ʃ/. Its voiced counterpart is /dʒ/.

This sound is described as an unvoiced palato-alveolar sibilant affricate. The blade of the tongue touches the roof of the mouth behind the alveolar ridge, while the front is arched upward toward the hard palate. You first stop the air flow entirely, then direct it toward the center of the tongue and release it through the mouth only, creating high-frequency turbulence. It is produced without vibrations of the vocal cords.

The most common spelling for this sound is *"ch"*. It can be found in different positions within the words listed below.

Initial Position - **ch**ain, **ch**air, **ch**alk, **ch**allenge, **ch**amber, **ch**amp, **ch**ampion, **ch**ance, **ch**ancellor, **ch**ange, **ch**annel, **ch**ant, **ch**apel, **ch**aplain, **ch**apter, **ch**arcoal, **ch**ard, **ch**arge, **ch**arity, **ch**arm, **ch**art, **ch**arter, **ch**ase, **ch**at, **ch**eap, **ch**eat, **ch**eck, **ch**eek, **ch**eer, **ch**eese, **ch**eque, **ch**erry, **ch**ess, **ch**est, **ch**ew, **ch**ick, **ch**icken, **ch**ief, **ch**ild, **ch**ildren, **ch**ill, **ch**imney, **ch**in, **Ch**ina, **ch**ip, **ch**ocolate, **ch**oice, **ch**oke, **ch**oose, **ch**op, **ch**ore, **ch**uck, **ch**uckle, **ch**ump, **ch**unk, **ch**urch

Middle Position - a**ch**ieve, ar**ch**er, ba**ch**elor, blea**ch**ers, bree**ch**es, en**ch**ant, ex**ch**ange, fran**ch**ise, lun**ch**eon, mer**ch**andise, mer**ch**ant, or**ch**ard, pur**ch**ase, prea**ch**er, Ri**ch**ard, tea**ch**er, tou**ch**base, trea**ch**ery

Final Position - approa**ch**, ar**ch**, atta**ch**, ba**ch**, bea**ch**, ben**ch**, besee**ch**, blea**ch**, bran**ch**, brea**ch**, bree**ch**, broo**ch**, brun**ch**, bun**ch**, chur**ch**, coa**ch**, cockroa**ch**, cou**ch**, crou**ch**, crun**ch**, deta**ch**, ea**ch**, hun**ch**, impea**ch**, in**ch**, laun**ch**, lea**ch**, lee**ch**, lun**ch**, mar**ch**, mu**ch**, ostri**ch**, ou**ch**, pea**ch**, per**ch**, pin**ch**, poa**ch**, por**ch**, pou**ch**, prea**ch**, pun**ch**, ran**ch**, rea**ch**, resear**ch**, ri**ch**, roa**ch**, scor**ch**, scree**ch**, sear**ch**, slou**ch**, spee**ch**, su**ch**, tea**ch**, tor**ch**, tou**ch**, tren**ch**, vou**ch**, whi**ch**

Curiously, the digraph "ch" can be pronounced either /tʃ/ or /dʒ/ in the following words.

sandwi**ch**, spina**ch**, Greenwi**ch**, Norwi**ch**

The letter combination *"tch"* also exhibits this sound.

> *batch, blotch, botch, butch, catch, clutch, crotch, crutch, dispatch, ditch, dutch, etch, fetch, fitch, glitch, hatch, hitch, hutch, itch, latch, match, notch, patch, pitch, rematch, retch, scotch, scratch, sketch, slitch, snatch, snitch, stitch, stretch, swatch, switch, thatch, twitch, unhitch, watch, witch, wretch, escutcheon, butcher, catcher, hatchet, ketchup, kitchen, pitcher, pitchfork, ratchet*

Conversely, the digraph *"ch"* is silent in the following word.

> *yacht*

In a similar fashion, the suffix *"-ture"* and derivative words always evoke /tʃ/.

> *adventure, aperture, architecture, capture, caricature, creature, culture, denture, departure, feature, fixture, fracture, furniture, future, gesture, juncture, lecture, literature, manufacture, mature, miniature, mixture, moisture, nature, nurture, overture, picture, posture, rupture, suture, structure, texture, temperature, vulture, architectural, cultural, gestural, natural, postural, structural*

In addition, /tʃ/ is present in the following suffixes containing *"t"* followed by *"u"*.

> *actual, conceptual, contextual, eventual, habitual, intel-*

> lectual, mutual, perpetual, punctual, ritual, spiritual, vir-
> tual, actually, eventually, virtually, statuary, usufructuary,
> voluptuary, actuate, accentuate, effectuate, fluctuate,
> habituate, perpetuate, punctuate, situate, accentuation,
> fluctuation, perpetuation, punctuation, situation, matu-
> rity, perpetuity, contemptuous, impetuous, incestuous,
> spirituous, virtuous

Furthermore, the digraph *"tu"* containing /tʃ/ is observed in the words below.

> century, spatula, titular, petulant, postulate, postulation,
> fortune, fortunate, statue, virtue, statute

The suffix *"-tion"* is normally pronounced with /ʃ/. However, when preceded by *"s"* the letter *"t"* is said /tʃ/.

> question, bastion, digestion, ingestion, egestion, com-
> bustion, congestion, exhaustion, suggestion, Christian,
> Sebastian

By the same token, you can exceptionally find *"t"* as /tʃ/ when followed by *"e"*.

> righteous, amateur

Lastly, there are a few words in which the letter *"c"* and digraphs display this sound.

> cello, concerto, cappuccino, capriccio, Czech

The following homophones contain the sound /tʃ/: _check_ - _cheque_ - _Czech_; _which_ - _witch_.

It is beneficial to know about the phonological process known as voicing or sonorization; in which a normally voiceless consonant becomes voiced when adjacent to voiced sounds. This commonly happens when speaking fast. The words listed below could demonstrate this phenomenon; with the voiceless /tʃ/ being voiced to /dʒ/.

> _approa**ch** this, atta**ch** themselves, ben**ch**mark, bun**ch** grass, ea**ch** breath, lun**ch**meat, mu**ch** longer, pea**ch** juice, ri**ch** man, ri**ch** woman, sear**ch**bar, spee**ch**less, su**ch** respect, tou**ch**base, tou**ch** me, whi**ch** direction, whi**ch** jewelry, whi**ch** version_

Please, don't forget to record yourself saying the words, compare it to the model and make any necessary corrections. It is advisable to repeat this exercise on a daily basis. Furthermore, consider writing and practicing with tongue twisters and sentences that emphasize the pronunciation of /tʃ/ in various topics and daily life scenarios.

dʒ
as in *job*

This phoneme represents the initial consonant sound in words such as *"joy" and "gym"*, and the final one in *"age" and "edge"*. It can be explained as a short /d/ sound right before and merged with /ʒ/. Its unvoiced counterpart is /tʃ/.

This sound is described as a voiced palato-alveolar sibilant affricate. The blade of the tongue touches the roof of the mouth behind the alveolar ridge, while the front is arched upward toward the hard palate. You first stop the air flow entirely, then direct it toward the center of the tongue and release it through the mouth only, creating high-frequency turbulence. The vocal cords vibrate during the articulation.

One common spelling for this sound is the letter *"j"*. The following words feature this spelling in different positions.

Initial Position - *jack, jacket, jade, jaguar, jail, jam, jar, jasmine, jaunt, jaunty, jaw, jay, jazz, Jamaica, James, Jane, January, Japan, jealous, jeans, jeep, jelly, jeopardy, jerk, jess, jet, jew, jewel, jewelry, jigger, jiggle, jigsaw, jingle, jinx, jitter, job, jockey, join, joint, joke, journal, journalism, journey, joy, Joe, John, Jones, Joseph, jubilee, judo, jug, jump, judge, juice, jump, junction, jungle, junior, junk, jury, just, justice, justify, juvenile, July, June*

Middle Position - *conjure, enjoy, inject, injection, injure, majestic, majesty, major, majority, object, perjure, project, prejudice, reject, subject, subjective, subjunctive, trajectory*

Additionally, the digraph "dj" is pronounced as /dʒ/.

adjacent, adjective, adjoin, adjourn, adjudicate, adjudge, adjunct, adjust, adjutant, adjutancy, Djakarta

On the other hand, the most common spelling for /dʒ/ is the letter "g" when followed by "e", "i" and even "y". In this case, "g" is known as soft "g". The words listed below contain this letter at the beginning.

"e" - *gee, gel, gelatine, gem, gender, gene, genera, general, generalize, generate, generation, generic, generosity, generous, genesis, genetic, genial, genie, genital, genius, genome, genocide, genotype, gentile, gentle, gentleman, genuine, geodesic, geography, geology, ge-*

ometry, *geriatrics, germ, germinate, gesticule, gesture, Genoa, Germany, George, Georgia*

"i" - *giant, giardia, gigabyte, gigantic, gin, ginger, gingiva, giraffe*

"y" - *gym, gymnast, gypsy, gyrate, gyroscope*

In the following words, the letter *"g"* appears in the middle.

"e" - *agency, agenda, algebra, allergen, analgesic, angel, apologetic, burgess, charger, collagen, congest, contingency, danger, detergent, digestion, diligent, divergent, dungeon, emergency, evangelical, exigent, ginger, heterogeneous, hydrogen, imagery, indigenous, indulgent, ingenuity, ingest, insurgent, intelligent, legend, longevity, manager, messenger, negligent, oxygen, pageant, passenger, progeny, pungent, refrigerator, refugee, regent, sergeant, stranger, surgery, tangent, teenager, tragedy, transgenic, urgent, vegetarian, vegetation, vengeance, pigeon, sturgeon, surgeon, advantageous, courageous, gorgeous, outrageous, Algeria, Angela, Argentina, Nigeria, Roger*

"i" - *agile, allegiant, allergic, angina, apologize, engine, engineer, digit, digital, eligible, fragile, frigid, hygiene, illegible, imagine, legislate, legit, legitimate, logic, longitude, longitudinal, magic, magistral, margin, nostalgia, original, regimen, register, rigid, surgical, tangible, trag-*

ic, vagina, vigil, vigilant, virgin, zoological, contagion, legion, region, religion, contagious, litigious, prestigious, Belgium, Georgia, Virginia

"y" - misogyny, allergy, analogy, anthology, apology, biology, cardiology, elegy, energy, etiology, eulogy, geology, gynecology, histology, ideology, lethargy, orgy, pathology, prodigy, psychology, stingy, strategy, technology, trilogy, virology, Egypt

You can oddly find this sound in "g" succeeded by "a" in these two examples.

algae, margarine

Furthemore, the letter "g" can be frequently seen at the end of words. It comes accompanied by the magic "e".

After Vowels - age, cage, engage, mage, page, rage, stage, wage, gauge, huge, refuge, oblige, prestige, siege, advantage, anchorage, average, baggage, bandage, bondage, carnage, cleavage, coinage, courage, coverage, damage, drainage, encourage, envisage, foliage, footage, garbage, haulage, hemorrhage, homage, image, language, leverage, lineage, luggage, manage, message, mortgage, orphanage, package, passage, plumage, postage, sausage, savage, sewage, storage, suffrage, vantage, village, vintage, voltage, voyage, carriage, marriage, miscarriage, college, privilege

After Consonants - *indulge, arrange, avenge, challenge, change, cringe, fringe, grange, hinge, lounge, orange, plunge, range, revenge, sponge, strange, syringe, charge, diverge, forge, gorge, large, merge, purge, scourge, urge, verge, George*

This next example contains a "*g*" + magic "*e*" in the middle of the word.

vegetable

Moreover, the double "*g*" is pronounced as /dʒ/ in a certain number of words.

suggest, suggestion, exaggerate, arpeggio, loggia, solfeggio, veggies

By the same token, the dipgraph "*dg*" is normally said /dʒ/.

budget, fidget, gadget, midget, widget, judgmental, acknowledge, adjudge, badge, bridge, budge, cartridge, dodge, edge, fridge, grudge, hedge, judge, knowledge, ledge, lodge, madge, patridge, pledge, porridge, ridge, sledge, smudge, wedge

In contrast, the letter "*d*" followed by "*u*" manifests /dʒ/ in the following words.

educate, education, graduate, graduation, adulate, modulate, fraudulent, pendulum, pendulous, procedure,

> *gradual, decidual, individual, residual, module, sched-*
> *ule, arduous, deciduous*

There are also these two words in which *"d"* sounds /dʒ/ but is followed by *"i"*.

> *cordial, soldier*

Besides, /dʒ/ can be found as *"t"* in the following words. However, it is regarded by some as informal or sloppy.

> *congratulate, congratulations*

Interestingly, the digraph *"ch"* can be pronounced either /tʃ/ or /dʒ/ in the few examples listed below.

> *sandwich, spinach, Greenwich, Norwich*

In addition, some minimal pairs between /tʃ/ and /dʒ/: H - *age, search - surge, batch - badge, rich - ridge.*

Last but not least, it is useful to know about the phonological process known as devoicing; in which a normally voiced consonant is replaced by a voiceless one when adjacent to unvoiced sounds. This commonly happens when speaking fast. The words listed below could exhibit this phenomenon; with the voiced /dʒ/ sound being devoiced to /tʃ/.

> *arrange for, change to, edge tool, garbage can, lounge*
> *chair, luggage cart, luggage tag, merge to*

Please, don't forget to record yourself saying the words, compare it to the model and make any necessary corrections. It is advisable to repeat this exercise on a daily basis. Furthermore, consider writing and practicing with tongue twisters and sentences that emphasize the pronunciation of /dʒ/ in various topics and daily life scenarios.

Chapter 9

Minimal Pairs

z *and* dʒ

The phoneme /dʒ/ is an explosive sound that bears similarities to /tʃ/, which resembles a sneeze and consequently it is almost impossible to sustain for a long time. In contrast, /z/ is a soft, vocalized version of /s/ and can be prolonged indefinitely.

bars - barge	grains - grange	strains - strange
bins - binge	guns - gunge	tins - tinge
buzz - budge	Mars - marge	was - wodge
chains - change	pays - page	ways - wage
chars - charge	purrs - purge	zag - jag
fours - forge	raise, rays - rage	zest - jest
frizz - fridge	seize, sees - siege	zig - jig
fuzz - fudge	sins - singe	zip - gip
gaze - gauge	stays - stage	

Chapter 10

f *as in* **feel**

This phoneme represents the initial consonant sound in words such as *"fast"* and *"foot"*, and the final one in *"wife"* and *"self"*. There are also a few words where it corresponds to *"gh"* as in *"cough"* or *"ph"* as in *"phone"*. Its voiced counterpart is /v/.

This sound is described as an unvoiced labiodental fricative. It is articulated with the lower lip and the upper teeth. You constrict the air flow through a narrow channel at the place of articulation, causing turbulence. The air is allowed to escape through the mouth only. It is produced without vibrations of the vocal cords.

The /f/ is most commonly spelled as *"f"*. It can be found in different positions.

Initial Position - *fabric, face, fact, fade, fail, faint, faith, fake, fall, false, fame, family, fan, fancy, fang, far, fare, farm, fart, fast, fat, fatal, fate, father, fax, fear, feast, feather, feature, fee, feed, feel, feet, fell, fellow, felony, female, fen, fence, fend, fertil, festive, fetch, feud, fever, few, fiber, fiddle, field, fifty, fight, file, fill, film, fin, final, find, fine, finger, fire, firm, first, fish, fist, fit, five, fix, focus, foe, fog, fold, folklore, follow, fond, font, food, fool, foot, for, four, force, forget, fork, form, forum, found, fox, fuel, full, fund, funny, fur, fuse, fuss, futile, future, flag, flake, flame, flare, flash, flask, flat, flavor, flaw, fleet, flesh, flex, flick, flight, flip, flirt, float, flock, flood, flop, floss, flow, flower, flu, fluent, fluid, flush, flute, fly, fragile, frame, frank, fraud, freak, freckle, freeze, frenzy, frequent, fresh, friction, fridge, friend, fright, fringe, frigid, frog, frolic, from, front, frost, froth, frozen, fructose, frugal, fruit, frustrate*

Middle Position - *infant, infarction, manufacture, surface, unfair, curfew, defeat, infect, prefer, refer, benefit, define, outfit, prefix, refine, significant, before, conform, comfort, inform, reform, therefore, infuse, refuge, refund, refuse, sulfur, deflate, inflate, inflex, reflect, rifle, stifle, trifle, refloat, seafloor, influence, reflux, butterfly, firefly, afraid, refract, refrain, carefree, refresh, girlfriend, infringe, confront, defrost, surfboard, briefcase, selfdom, Afghanistan, surfman, deafness, after, craft, draft, gift, graft, left, lift, shift, soft, swift*

Final Position - *deaf, leaf, loaf, oaf, beef, belief, brief,* chef, chief, reef, relief, thief, if, proof, roof, elf, golf, self, shelf, wolf, barf, dwarf, scarf, snarf, surf

Magic "e" - chafe, safe, knife, life, rife, strife, wife

In addition, the double "f" is a frequent spelling for "f".

Middle Position - affable, affair, buffalo, affect, buffer, buffet, coffee, differ, different, effect, effective, offend, offer, suffer, affirm, coffin, difficult, efficient, graffiti, muffin, office, official, suffix, traffic, afford, chiffon, effort, suffocate, baffle, muffle, raffle, ruffle, scuffle, shuffle, sniffle, waffle, affront, riffraff, suffrage

Final Position - chaff, gaff, staff, cliff, sheriff, sniff, stiff, whiff, off, scoff, bluff, duff, cuff, huff, puff, stuff, riff-raff, giraffe

Interestingly, in the following words, the letter "f" is next to a silent letter.

calf, half, behalf, often, soften

On the other hand, the digraph "ph" is another typical spelling for /f/.

Initial Position - phantom, pharmacy, pharynx, phase, pheasant, phenix, phenomenon, philology, philosophy, phimosis, phobia, phone, phoneme, phonetics, phosphor, *photo*, *photon*, *physical*, *physician*, *physics*, *phys-iology*, *phlebitis*, *phlegm*, *phrase*, *phreatic*, *phrenic*

Middle Position - al*pha*, al*pha*bet, as*pha*lt, cello*pha*ne, ele*pha*nt, em*pha*sis, epi*pha*ny, or*pha*n, apostro*phe*, at-mos*phe*re, blas*phe*my, catastro*phe*, ci*phe*r, e*phe*drine, e*phe*meral, go*phe*r, hy*phe*n, ne*phe*w, pro*phe*cy, *proph*-et, s*phe*re, stro*phe*, am*phi*bian, dol*phi*n, endor*phi*n, gra*phi*c, gra*phi*te, hemo*phi*lia, mor*phi*ne, neutro*phi*l, pe-do*phi*le, so*phi*sticate, s*phi*ncter, am*pho*ra, eu*pho*ny, eu-*pho*ria, lym*pho*cyte, meta*pho*r, mor*pho*logy, phos*pho*r, saxo*pho*ne, si*pho*n, so*pho*more, sym*pho*ny, tele*pho*ne, ty*pho*on, as*phy*xia, atro*phy*, biogra*phy*, em*phy*sema, epi*phy*sis, geogra*phy*, philoso*phy*, photogra*phy*, tro*phy*, pam*phl*et, a*phr*odisiac, A*phr*odite, dia*phr*agm, epine*phr*-ine, herma*phr*odite, ne*phr*on, di*ph*thong, mono*ph*thong

Final Position - epita*ph*, gra*ph*, autogra*ph*, diagra*ph*, para-gra*ph*, photogra*ph*, mor*ph*, dimor*ph*, lym*ph*, nym*ph*, tri-um*ph*, Jose*ph*

Furthermore, the letter combination *"pph"* exhibits this sound.

sa*pph*ire, sa*pph*ic

Lastly, there are some words containing /f/ as *"gh"*.

cou*gh*, trou*gh*, lau*gh*, lau*gh*ter, drau*gh*t, enou*gh*, rou*gh*, slou*gh*, tou*gh*

Please, don't forget to record yourself saying the words, compare it to the model and make any necessary corrections. It is advisable to repeat this exercise on a daily basis. Furthermore, consider writing and practicing with tongue twisters and sentences that emphasize the pronunciation of /f/ in various topics and daily life scenarios.

Chapter 11

V

as in *very*

T his phoneme represents the initial consonant sound in words such as *"verb"*, *"vacation"* and *"voice"*, and the final one in *"above"* and *"love"*. Its unvoiced counterpart is /f/.

This sound is described as a voiced labiodental fricative. It is articulated with the lower lip and the upper teeth. You constrict the air flow through a narrow channel at the place of articulation, causing turbulence. The air is allowed to escape through the mouth only. The vocal cords vibrate during the articulation.

The /v/ is normally spelled *"v"* as it can be observed in the following words.

Initial Position - **v**acant, **v**acancy, **v**acation, **v**accine, **v**acuum, **v**aginal, **v**ain, **v**alid, **v**alley, **v**alue, **v**ampire, **v**an,

vandalism, **v**anguard, **v**anilla, **v**anity, **v**ariable, **v**ariety, **v**ary, **v**ascular, **v**ast, **v**ault, **v**egetable, **v**ehicle, **v**ein, **v**elvet, **v**endetta, **v**endor, **v**enereal, **v**entilate, **v**enture, **v**enue, **v**erb, **v**erdict, **v**erify, **v**ermin, **v**ersatile, **v**erse, **v**ersion, **v**ersus, **v**ertebral, **v**ertical, **v**ery, **v**est, **v**eteran, **v**eterinary, **v**ia, **v**ibe, **v**ibrant, **v**ibrate, **v**ice, **v**ictim, **v**ictor, **v**ictory, **v**ideo, **v**iew, **v**igorous, **v**illage, **v**indicate, **v**inegar, **v**intage, **v**iolate, **v**iolence, **v**iolet, **v**iolin, **v**irgin, **v**irtual, **v**irus, **v**ision, **v**isit, **v**ital, **v**itamin, **v**ivid, **v**ocabulary, **v**ocal, **v**ocalist, **v**ocation, **v**oice, **v**oid, **v**olcano, **v**olleyball, **v**olt, **v**oltage, **v**olume, **v**olunteer, **v**omit, **v**ote, **v**owel, **v**ulgar, **v**ulnerable

Middle Position - acti**v**ate, acti**v**ity, ad**v**ance, ad**v**antage, ad**v**enture, alle**v**iate, a**v**ailable, a**v**alanche, a**v**enue, a**v**erage, a**v**oid, beha**v**ior, cal**v**ary, ci**v**il, con**v**ent, con**v**ict, co**v**en, co**v**er, de**v**elop, de**v**il, di**v**erse, di**v**ert, ele**v**ate, e**v**en, e**v**ent, e**v**ening, e**v**er, e**v**idence, e**v**olve, fa**v**or, go**v**ernment, gra**v**ity, Har**v**ard, har**v**est, ha**v**oc, hea**v**en, how-e**v**er, indi**v**idual, inno**v**ate, in**v**ent, in**v**ert, in**v**est, in**v**olve, i**v**y, la**v**ish, le**v**el, li**v**er, li**v**id, Lou**v**re, lo**v**er, maneu**v**er, moti**v**ate, na**v**el, na**v**y, ner**v**ous, ne**v**er, no**v**el, obli**v**ious, ob**v**ious, o**v**er, per**v**ert, pi**v**ot, pi**v**otal, pre**v**ent, pre**v**iew, pri**v**ate, pro**v**erb, pro**v**ide, ra**v**el, ra**v**en, rele**v**ant, reser**v**ation, re**v**enue, ri**v**al, ri**v**er, ro**v**er, sa**v**age, sa**v**ior, ser**v**ant, ser**v**er, ser**v**ice, ser**v**ile, se**v**en, se**v**ere, sil**v**er, sur**v**ive, tra**v**el, tri**v**ial, uni**v**erse, vel**v**et, vi**v**id

Final Position - abo**ve**, achie**ve**, ali**ve**, arri**ve**, beha**ve**, belie**ve**, bra**ve**, car**ve**, ca**ve**, conser**ve**, co**ve**, cur**ve**, decei**ve**, *derive, deserve, dive, dove, drive, eve, evolve, five, give, grave, grieve, grove, groove, have, heave, hive, improve, involve, leave, live, love, move, naive, nerve, observe, olive, pave, prove, rave, receive, remove, re-trieve, save, serve, shove, slave, sleeve, solve, starve, stove, strive, survive, thrive, twelve, wave, weave, abu-sive, aggressive, comprehensive, decisive, defensive, erosive, evasive, excessive, exclusive, expensive, inva-sive, massive, passive, pensive, active, alternative, at-tractive, creative, effective, executive, initiative, motive, narrative, native, negative, positive, relative, selective*

The words below have a silent "e" following "v", making the phonetic sequence /vr/.

every, several, sovereign

Additionally, some nouns ending in "f" undergo a voicing or sonorization process, which changes the unvoiced /f/ to a voiced /v/, when forming their verb pairs.

belief - believe, shelf - shelve, grief - grieve, life - live, proof - prove, strife - strive, thief - thieve

Same occurs when some singular nouns ending in "f" form their plural.

beef - beeves, behalf - behalves, calf - calves, dwarf - dwarves, elf - elves, grief - grieves, half - halves, hoof - hooves, knife - knives, leaf - leaves, life - lives, loaf -

loaves, roof - rooves, scarf - scarves, self - selves, sheaf - sheaves, shelf - shelves, staff - staves, thief - thieves, wife - wives, wolf - wolves

In the same way, the double "v" maintains the /v/ sound.

navvy, savvy

Furthermore, these following words present the /v/ sound spelled as "f" and "ph".

of, nephew, Stephen

It is useful to know about the phonological process known as devoicing; in which a normally voiced consonant is replaced by a voiceless one when adjacent to unvoiced sounds. This commonly happens when speaking fast. The words listed below could exhibit this phenomenon; with the voiced /v/ being devoiced to /f/.

have to, of course, out of control

Please, don't forget to record yourself saying the words, compare it to the model and make any necessary corrections. It is advisable to repeat this exercise on a daily basis. Furthermore, consider writing and practicing with tongue twisters and sentences that emphasize the pronunciation of /v/ in various topics and daily life scenarios.

Chapter 12

Minimal Pairs

f and v

The sounds /f/ and /v/ are articulated using a similar mouth position, with the top teeth lightly touching the bottom lip. However, the sound /f/ is produced with a stronger expulsion of air, without engaging the vocal cords.

belief - believe	fee - V	foist - voiced
chaff - chav	feel - veal	foul - vowel
duff - dove	feign - vain, vein	fox - vox
fail - veil	fender - vendor	gif - give
fan - van	ferry - very	grief - grieve
fast - vast	fie - vie	guff - guv
fat - vat	file - vile	half - halve
fault - vault	fine - vine	leaf - leave
fear - veer	foal - vole	life - live

off - of   safe - save   surf - serve

proof - prove   skiff - skiv   waif - waive

reef - reeve   strife - strive

θ

as in **thing**

This phoneme represents the consonant sound in words such as *"think"*, *"thanks"* and *"north"*. The spelling for /θ/ is always the digraph *"th"*. Its voiced counterpart is /ð/.

This sound is described as an unvoiced dental non-sibilant fricative. The tip or the blade of the tongue is positioned at the upper teeth. It is often produced with the tongue between the upper and lower teeth, which is known as interdental. You direct the airstream along the center of the tongue and constrict it through a narrow channel at the place of articulation, causing turbulence. The air is allowed to escape through the mouth only. It is produced without vibrations of the vocal cords.

The words listed below present the /θ/ followed by vowel sounds in different positions.

Initial Position - *thank, thatch, thaw, theater, theft, thematic, theme, theorem, theory, therapy, thermic, thermometer, thesaurus, thesis, thick, thief, thieve, thigh, thimble, thin, thing, think, third, thirteen, thirst, thirty, thistle, thong, thorn, thorough, thought, thousand, thug, thumb, thump, thunder, thunk, Thursday, thyroid*

Middle Position - *anything, everything, nothing, something, aesthetic, amphitheater, anesthesia, anthem, anthology, antipathy, antithesis, apathy, apothecary, atheism, atheist, authentic, author, authority, brothel, catharsis, catheter, cathode, catholic, diphtheria, diphthong, empathy, enthuse, enthusiasm, epithelium, ethanol, ethereal, ethic, euthanasia, hawthorn, healthy, hypothesis, idiopathic, lethal, lethargy, lithium, marathon, mathematics, methane, method, orthodox, orthography, ophthalmology, panther, parenthesis, pathetic, plethora, python, strengthen, sympathy, synthesis, without, Dorothy, Ethiopia, Martha*

Alternatively, the /θ/ is followed by consonant sounds in the next words.

Initial Position - *thrall, thrash, thread, threat, three, threesome, thresh, threw, thrice, thrift, thrill, thrive, throat, thrombosis, throne, throttle, through, throughout, throw, thrum, thrush, thrust*

Middle Position - *anthrax, anthropology, arthralgia, ar-*

> *thritis, bathrobe, bathroom, philanthropy, athlete, ruthless, triathlon, bathtub, breathtaking, arithmetic, birthday, earthquake, ethnic, mouthpiece*

You can also find the *"th"* at the end of words, even with the magic *"e"*.

> *aftermath, bath, beneath, bequeath, birth, both, breath, broth, cloth, death, depth, earth, faith, filth, forth, froth, growth, heath, health, hearth, hath, hyacinth, labyrinth, length, loath, math, mirth, month, moth, mouth, myth, north, oath, path, rath, ruth, sheath, sleuth, sloth, smith, south, stealth, strength, synth, teeth, tooth, truth, warmth, wealth, width, worth, wrath, wreath, youth, Goliath, absinthe*

Distinctively, the *"th"* is utilized to create ordinal numbers by adding it as a suffix to cardinal numbers.

> *fourth, fifth, sixth, seventh, eighth, ninth, tenth, eleventh, twelfth, thirteenth...*

In a similar fashion, when the cardinal number ends in *"y"*, the suffix *"-eth"* is added instead.

> *twentieth, thirtieth, fortieth, fiftieth, sixtieth, seventieth, eightieth, ninetieth*

On the other hand, the words below can be pronounced with either /θ/ or /ð/.

booth, with, within, without

These two words contain a silent *"th"* in their spelling.

asthma, isthmus

Finally, *"threw"* and *"through"* are homophones featuring /θ/.

> Please, don't forget to record yourself saying the words, compare it to the model and make any necessary corrections. It is advisable to repeat this exercise on a daily basis. Furthermore, consider writing and practicing with tongue twisters and sentences that emphasize the pronunciation of /θ/ in various topics and daily life scenarios.

ð

as in **there**

T his phoneme represents the consonant sound in words such as *"the"*, *"father"* and *"smooth"*. The spelling for /ð/ is always the digraph *"th"*. Its unvoiced counterpart is /θ/.

This sound is described as a voiced dental non-sibilant fricative. The tip or the blade of the tongue is positioned at the upper teeth. It is often produced with the tongue between the upper and lower teeth, which is known as interdental. You direct the airstream along the center of the tongue and constrict it through a narrow channel at the place of articulation, causing turbulence. The air is allowed to escape through the mouth only. The vocal cords vibrate during the articulation.

Let's start by reviewing the spelling for this sound in different positions.

Initial Position - *the, that, those, this, these, than, then, they, their, them, though, thus, there, therefore, there-after, thereby, therefrom, therein, thereof, thereupon, thence, thou, thee, thy, thine, thyself*

Middle Position - *although, other, another, either, neither, rather, whether, together, altogether, arrhythmia, both-er, brother, brethren, clothing, dither, father, farther, fathom, feather, further, furthermore, gather, heathen, heather, hither, lather, leather, mother, nether, Neth-erlands, nevertheless, nonetheless, northern, pother, slither, smithereens, southern, swarthy, thither, weath-er, withdraw, worthy*

Final Position - *smooth, bequeath, betroth*

In addition, it can be visualized at the end of words followed by the magic "e".

blithe, lithe, scathe, scythe, seethe, soothe, swathe, writhe

Interestingly, some nouns ending in "th" undergo a voicing or sonorization process, which changes the unvoiced /θ/ to a voiced /ð/, when forming their verb pairs. The magic "e" is commonly added.

bath - bathe, breath - breathe, cloth - clothe, lath - lathe, loath - loathe, mouth - mouth, sheath - sheathe, teeth - teethe, wreath - wreathe

Furthermore, when the letter combination *"-thm"* appears at the end of a word, a reduced vowel sound /ə/ is pronounced between /ð/ and /m/.

> *algorith(ə)m, logarith(ə)m, rhyth(ə)m*

There are some irregular plurals of nouns ending in /θ/ that are pronounced as /ðz/.

> *baths, booths, mouths, oaths, paths, truths, wreaths, youths*

On the other hand, the words below can be pronounced with either /θ/ or /ð/.

> *booth, with, within, without*

These two words contain a silent *"th"* in their spelling.

> *asthma, isthmus*

Finally, it is useful to know about the phonological process known as devoicing; in which a normally voiced consonant is replaced by a voiceless one when adjacent to unvoiced sounds. This commonly happens when speaking fast. The words listed below could exhibit this phenomenon; with the voiced /ð/ sound being devoiced to /θ/.

> *breathe through, smooth shift*

Please, don't forget to record yourself saying the words, compare it to the model and make any necessary corrections. It is advisable to repeat this exercise on a daily basis. Furthermore, consider writing and practicing with tongue twisters and sentences that emphasize the pronunciation of /ð/ in various topics and daily life scenarios.

Chapter 15

Minimal Pairs

S and θ

The phoneme /θ/ is articulated with the tongue placed between the teeth or slightly sticking out from the mouth. In contrast, /s/ is pronounced with the tongue positioned further back and the mouth opened wider.

face - faith	piss - pith
force - fourth	race - wraith
gross - growth	sank - thank
mass - math	saw - thaw
miss - myth	seam, seem - theme
moss - moth	sick - thick
mouse - mouth	sigh - thigh
Norse - North	sin - thin
pass - path	sing - thing

sink - **th**ink

some - **th**umb

song - **th**ong

sought - **th**ought

sum - **th**umb

sump - **th**ump

symbol - **th**imble

ten**s**e - ten**th**

truce - tru**th**

u**s**e - you**th**

wor**s**e - wor**th**

Chapter 16

Minimal Pairs

f *and* θ

The sounds /f/ and /θ/ are made just by blowing out air without using your voice. /f/ is similar to /θ/ but with the tongue inside the mouth, while /θ/ has the tongue between or even sticking out of the teeth. One way to practice the /θ/ sound is by ensuring that your tongue makes contact with a finger positioned on your lips.

deaf - death	first - thirst	frill - thrill
duff - doth	fought - thought	fro - throw
fang - thang	free - three	froze - throws
fawn - thorn	freeze - threes	fug - thug
fief - thief	fresh - thresh	furred - third
fin - thin	fret - threat	oaf - oath
firm - therm	frieze - threes	trough - troth

Chapter 17

Minimal Pairs

Z and ð

Both /ð/ and /θ/ are similar sounds pronounced with the tongue touching or between the teeth. To practice, stick your tongue out of your mouth and ensure it gets moist in front of a mirror or with a finger. /ð/ is voiced and can be confused with /z/, which is pronounced similarly with vocal cords and spread lips. However, /z/ has the tongue well inside the mouth and the lips are spread thinner and wider.

baize, bays - bathe	*lies - lithe*
breeze - breathe	*lows - loathe*
close - clothe	*she's - sheathe*
closing - clothing	*sighs, size - scythe*
C's, seas, sees - seethe	*sues - soothe*
laze - lathe	*teas - teethe*

teasing - teething
ties - tithe

T's - teethe
whizz - with

k

as in **king**

This phoneme represents the initial consonant sound in words such as *"king"*, *"cat"* and *"quick"*, and the final one in *"look"*, *"luck"* and *" basic"*. Its voiced counterpart is /g/.

This sound is described as an unvoiced velar plosive. The back of the tongue contacts the soft palate and blocks the airflow entirely in both the vocal and nasal tracts. Then the articulators are separated, releasing the compressed air through the mouth only. It is produced without vibrations of the vocal cords.

/k/ is typically spelled with the letter *"k"*, which can be observed in the following words.

Initial Position - **k**angaroo, **K**ansas, **k**arate, **k**arma, **k**ayak, **k**eep, **k**ennel, **k**ey, **k**ick, **k**id, **k**ill, **k**ind, **k**ing, **k**iss, **k**it, **k**itchen, **k**oala, **K**orea, **k**laxon, **K**leenex, **K**remlin, **k**rypton

Middle Position - *skeleton, skeptic, skill, skim, skin, skip, sky, okay, remarkable, donkey, monkey, Nike, turkey, baker, speaker, worker, market, naked, bikini, haiku, cranky, funky, husky, inky, leaky, murky, risky, ankle, sparkle, wrinkle, Oklahoma, chakra, books, breaks, cooks, looks, thanks, walks, weeks, asks, desks, husks, masks, tasks, bookstore*

Final Position - *ask, husk, mask, risk, task, bleak, book, break, dark, cook, cork, creek, crook, fork, freak, look, milk, oak, park, peak, pink, pork, shark, sink, soak, speak, week, work.* The words *"folk", "yolk", "chalk", "stalk", "talk", "walk"* and *"caulk"* have a silent *"l".*

Magic *"e"* - *bake, bike, cake, duke, fake, hike, joke, lake, like, make, nuke, rake, shake, smoke, snake, sake, take, wake, woke*

It can also appear as a double *"k".*

Hanukkah, trekking

By the same token, the digraph *"ck"* is frequently used for /k/.

Middle Position - *cracker, hacker, bracket, bucket, cricket, jacket, picket, pocket, racket, rocket, ticket, beckon, gecko, hickory, reckon, buckle, chuckle, crackle, fickle, heckle, knuckle, pickle, shackle, sickle, tackle, tickle, attacks, clocks, locks, packs, rocks, socks, backstage*

Final Position - atta**ck**, ba**ck**, bla**ck**, cra**ck**, ha**ck**, la**ck**, pa**ck**, sna**ck**, tra**ck**, be**ck**, che**ck**, de**ck**, fle**ck**, ne**ck**, pe**ck**, spe**ck**, wre**ck**, bri**ck**, cli**ck**, ki**ck**, li**ck**, pi**ck**, qui**ck**, si**ck**, sti**ck**, tri**ck**, thi**ck**, blo**ck**, clo**ck**, do**ck**, flo**ck**, kno**ck**, lo**ck**, mo**ck**, ro**ck**, so**ck**, sho**ck**, bu**ck**, chu**ck**, du**ck**, lu**ck**, plu**ck**, mu**ck**, stu**ck**, tru**ck**

Similarly, you can find the sound /k/ as *"kh"* in a few loanwords.

khaki, **Kh**alifa, **Kh**rushchev, shei**kh**

It is worth reviewing the following words containing a silent *"k"* preceding *"n"*, which indicates a Germanic origin of the words.

knack, **k**nead, **k**nee, **k**neel, **k**new, **k**nickers, **k**nife, **k**night, **k**nit, **k**nob, **k**nock, **k**not, **k**now, **k**nowledge, **k**nuckle

On the other hand, you may observe /k/ spelled *"c"* in numerous words, which is known as hard *"c"* and is considered the most common spelling for /k/ at the beginning of words. This occurs when *"c"* is followed by the vowels *"a"*, *"o"* or *"u"* and consonants.

Before *"a"* - **c**ake, **c**all, **c**ap, **c**ar, **c**ard, **c**arpet, **c**arry, **c**ash, **c**at, **c**atch, s**c**ale, s**c**am, de**c**ade, edu**c**ation, es**c**ape, peli**c**an, mimi**c**al, traffi**c**able

Before *"o"* - **c**oat, **c**oin, **c**ome, **c**onfuse, **c**ook, **c**ool, **c**ork, **c**orn, **c**orner, **c**ot, **c**ourt, **c**over, s**c**old, s**c**oundrel, a**c**oustic, ba**c**on, e**c**onomy, heli**c**opter

Before "u" - cub, cucumber, cue, culture, cup, curtain, curve, cushion, cut, cute, sculpture, articulate, biscuit, focus, peculiar, security, vacuum

Before "l" - clam, clap, clean, click, clip, climb, clock, clown, club, clue, clinic, declare, incline, include, nuclear, article, barnacle, circle, cycle, miracle, particle, obstacle, uncle, vehicle, magical, medical, musical, physical

Before "r" - crab, crack, crash, crate, crawl, cream, create, credit, creep, crew, crib, cringe, crisp, critic, crook, crop, cross, crow, crowd, cry, crystal, crypt, scrap, scream, script, scrimmage, across, democracy, lucrative, massacre, mediocre, microscope, sacrifice, secret

Other Consonants - act, construct, direct, fact, predict, action, activity, collective, doctor, election, galactic, picture, sanction, sanctify, sanctimonious, sanctuary, sanctum, section, selective, critics, docs, mathematics, mimics, panics, picnics, plastics, politics, statistics, topics, traffics, facsimile

The letter "c" also produces /k/ at the end of the word.

academic, attic, basic, classic, clinic, comic, cosmic, economic, epic, frolic, garlic, graphic, havoc, logic, maniac, mimic, music, panic, picnic, public, relic, specific, topic, traffic, tragic

Interestingly, a "k" is added to certain words ending in "c" when expanded with a suffix.

frolicked, mimicked, panicked, picnicked, trafficked

Mirroring the letter "c", the digraph "cc" also produces this sound.

buccaneer, desiccate, impeccable, moccasins, occasion, staccato, accolade, accommodate, accompany, accomplish, accord, accordion, accost, account, broccoli, Morocco, raccoon, succor, tobacco, accumulate, accurate, accuse, hiccup, occupy, occur, succumb, acclaim, acclimate, ecclesiastic, occlude, accredit, accrue

The "cc" followed by "e" is oddly pronounced /k/ in the next word.

soccer

Used much less frequently, "ch" represents this sound in words of Greek origin.

Initial Position - **ch**ameleon, **ch**amomile, **ch**aos, **ch**aotic, **ch**aracter, **ch**aracteristic, **ch**arisma, **ch**arismatic, **ch**asm, **ch**emical, **ch**emist, **ch**emistry, **ch**imera, **ch**oir, **ch**olera, **ch**olesterol, **ch**oral, **ch**ord, **ch**oreography, **ch**orus, **ch**lorine, **Ch**loe, **Ch**ris, **Ch**ristmas, **ch**rome, **ch**romatic, **ch**ronic, **ch**ronicle, **ch**ronology

Middle Position - a**ch**alasia, A**ch**illes, al**ch**emy, anar**ch**y, an**ch**or, ar**ch**aic, ar**ch**ive, ar**ch**ipelago, ar**ch**itect, ar**ch**eology, bronchial, bronchitis, dichotomy, echo, hierarchy, lichen, masochism, masochistic, matriarchy, mechanic, mechanism, melancholy, menarche, monarchy, ocher, oligarchy, orchestra, orchid, patriarchy, psyche, psychiatry, psychology, schedule, scheme, school, synchronize, tachicardia, technical, technician, technology, technique, trachea, matriarchs, monarchs, patriarchs, stomachs, Dachshund

Final Position - ache, epoch, matriarch, monarch, patriarch, stomach, tech

In addition, /k/ has a representation with the combination "cch".

zucchini

In English the letter "q" is always followed by "u". For most words, the pronunciation of "qu" forms the sequence /kw/.

Initial Position - quack, quaff, quake, qualify, quality, qualm, quandary, quantify, quantity, quark, quarrel, quarter, quash, queen, quell, quench, query, question, quick, quid, quill, quilt, quirk, quit, quiet, quite, quiver, quiz, quora, quota, quote, quotient

Middle Position - aqua, banquet, barbeque, bequeath, consequence, eloquence, enquire, equal, equip, equipment, exquisite, frequent, inquest, inquire, liquid, marquess, request, require, sequel, sequence, sequin, solil-

> *oquy, squad, squalid, squander, square, squash, squat,*
> *squeak, squeal, squelch, squeeze, squid, squint, squire,*
> *squirm, squirt, tranquil, tranquility, turquoise, ubiquitous*

Conversely, there are a few loanwords from other languages, mostly French, in which the *"qu"* sounds like /k/ without the /w/.

> Middle Position - *bouquet, croquet, sobriquet, tourniquet,*
> *communiqué, risqué, briquette, etiquette, conquer, li-*
> *queur, liquor, masquerade, mosquito*

> Magic *"e"* - *antique, boutique, casque, critique, mys-*
> *tique, oblique, physique, pique, technique, unique,*
> *burlesque, grotesque, picturesque, Romanesque, ba-*
> *roque, marque, mosque, opaque, plaque*

Curiously, the word below presents the /k/ represented by *"que"*.

> *queue*

In the same way, you may encounter some words with *"cqu"* said as /kw/.

> *acquaint, acquaintance, acquiesce, acquire, acquit,*
> *Macquarie*

On the flip side, the word below exhibits the *"cqu"* pronounced with /k/ without /w/.

> *lacquer*

Nevertheless, there are some exceptions in which the letter "q" is not followed by "u". The majority of these are anglicized from Arabic, Chinese and other languages.

> *tranq, qwerty, coq, jelq, niqab, Qatar, Qatari, Iraq, Iraqi, Iqaluit*

The "x", "xc" and "cc" spellings are pronounced as /ks/ in the following words.

> *box, complex, fax, fix, fox, flex, hoax, matrix, mix, ox, pox, relax, tax, wax, jinx, lynx, next, text, exclude, Oxford, exhale, experience, extend, approximate, axel, galaxy, maximum, taxi, excel, excellent, except, excess, excited, accent, accept, access, accident, eccentric, success*

In a similar fashion, "x" is pronounced /kʃ/ in the words below.

> *sexual, sexuality, bisexual, anxious, noxious, obnoxious, complexion, crucifixion, flexion*

It is beneficial to know about the phonological process known as voicing or sonorization; in which a normally voiceless consonant becomes voiced when adjacent to voiced sounds. This commonly happens when speaking fast. The words listed below often exhibit this phenomenon; with the voiceless /k/ sound being voiced to /g/.

> *backlash, bankrupt, black dog, blockbuster, clickbait, clockwise, dark meat, folk dance, folk music, likewise,*

lockdown, look brave, look like, oakwood, pink gun, risk war, sickness, speak now, truck driver, weekday, work-bench, workbook, workday, workload, work with

Please, don't forget to record yourself saying the words, compare it to the model and make any necessary corrections. It is advisable to repeat this exercise on a daily basis. Furthermore, consider writing and practicing with tongue twisters and sentences that emphasize the pronunciation of /k/ in various topics and daily life scenarios.

g

as in *get*

This phoneme represents the initial consonant sound in words such as *"go"* and *"target"*, and the final one in *"bag"*, *"egg"* and *"colleague"*. Its unvoiced counterpart is /k/.

This sound is described as a voiced velar plosive. The back of the tongue contacts the soft palate and blocks the airflow entirely in both the vocal and nasal tracts. Then the articulators are separated, releasing the compressed air through the mouth only. The vocal cords vibrate during the articulation.

Let's start by exploring the most common spelling for this sound, the letter *"g"*, which is known as hard *"g"* and often precedes the letters *"a"*, *"o"* or *"u"* and consonants.

Initial Position - **gag, gallon, gallery, gallop, game, garage, garbage, garden, garlic, gargle, gargoyle, gas, gas-**

oline, gate, gauge, gave, gay, go, goal, goat, goblin, god, gold, golf, good, goose, gore, gorilla, gossip, got, gothic, gouge, gourd, govern, gown, guff, gull, gullet, gum, gun, gurgle, gut, glacial, glad, glade, glamor, glance, gland, glare, glass, gleam, glee, glimpse, glitch, globe, gloom, gloss, glove, glow, glucose, glum, grab, grace, gram, grand, grant, grape, grass, grave, gray, great, grease, green, grid, grill, grind, grip, groan, grocery, gross, group, ground, grub, grudge, gruel, grump, grunt

Middle Position - again, alligator, elegant, gigantic, illegal, magazine, mortgage, obligate, organization, regard, sugar, ago, agony, bigot, bingo, dragon, ego, ergo, gargoyle, lagoon, mango, rigor, wagon, argue, August, figure, regular, afterglow, anglo, burglar, igloo, neglect, piglet, angle, eagle, gargle jungle, mingle, single, strangle, tangle, triangle, agree, degrade, diagram, hungry, Instagram, migrate, program, regret, vagrant, rugby, amygdala, bagful, augment, dogma, enigma, figment, fragment, magma, pigment, segment, stigma, cognate, diagnose, dignity, ignite, ignore, magnet, magnificent, recognize, signal, signify, jigsaw, dogtooth, pigtail, zigzag

Final Position - bag, brag, drag, fag, flag, gag, lag, rag, tag, wag, zigzag, beg, keg, leg, peg, big, dig, fig, gig, pig, rig, twig, wig, backlog, blog, bog, catalog, clog, cog, dog, fog, frog, hedgehog, hog, jog, log, smog, snog, tog, bug, drug, hug, jug, mug, plug, rug, shrug, slug, smug, snug, thug, renege

In words of Germanic origin, loanwords from other languages and irregular Greco-Latinate words, the sound /g/ may appear before the letters "e", "i" or "y" as well.

> Initial Position - *gear, gecko, geese, geld, get, gewgaw, geyser, gibbon, gibbous, giddy, gift, gig, giggle, gild, gill, gilt, gird, girder, girdle, girl, girth, git, give, gizmo, gizzard, gynecology*
>
> Middle Position - *burger, eager, finger, forget, target, tiger, together, begin, forgive*

In the same way, the double "g" is pronounced /g/ in the middle and end of words.

> Middle Position - *beggar, baggage, dagger, luggage, stagger, toboggan, trigger, agglomerate, agglutinate, gaggle, giggle, juggle, smuggle, snuggle, struggle, wiggle, wriggle, aggress, aggressive, aggregate, aggravate, aggrieve, eggplant*
>
> Final Position - *egg, hogg*

Additionally, the words listed below contain the letter "g" followed by "e" and "y". However, they are derived words in which the "g" is doubled to form another syllable.

> *bagger, bigger, biggest, digger, jogger, baggy, buggy, doggy, foggy, leggy, muggy, piggy*

The spelling *"gu"* forms the phonetic sequence /gw/ in a restricted number of words, most of them loanwords from other languages.

> **g**uacamole, **G**uam, **G**uatemala, **g**uava, i**g**uana, ja**g**uar, lan**g**uage, lin**g**ual, Mana**g**ua, Nicara**g**ua, Para**g**uay, Uru**g**uay, an**g**uish, distin**g**uish, lin**g**uist, lin**g**uistic, pen**g**uin, san**g**uine, san**g**uineous

In contrast, *"gu"* is more often pronounced just /g/, even at the end of words with a magic *"e"*.

> Initial Position - **gu**arantee, **gu**ard, **gu**ardian, **gu**ess, **gu**est, **gu**ernsey, **gu**ide, **gu**ild, **gu**ile, **gu**illotine, **gu**ilt, **gu**ilty, **gu**ise, **gu**itar, **Gu**inea, **gu**y
>
> Middle Position - ba**gu**ette, be**gu**ile, den**gue**, dis**gu**ise, lan**gu**or, mar**gu**erite, Portu**gu**ese, ro**gu**ish, un**gu**arded, van**gu**ard
>
> Magic *"e"* - analo**gue**, dialo**gue**, epilo**gue**, homolo**gue**, monolo**gue**, prolo**gue**, collea**gue**, lea**gue**, fati**gue**, intri**gue**, pla**gue**, va**gue**, mor**gue**, ro**gue**, vo**gue**, fu**gue**

Similarly, you can find the sound /g/ in the spelling *"gh"* in a few words.

> **gh**astly, **gh**ee, **gh**etto, **gh**ost, **gh**ostly, **gh**oul, **gh**oulish, Af**gh**anistan

On the other hand, there are multiple words having a silent *"g"*.

> *gnarl, gnarly, gnaw, gnome, gnu, align, sign, assign, consign, design, resign, benign, malign, arraign, campaign, champagne, deign, feign, reign, foreign, sovereign, coign, poignant, cologne, diaphragm, syntagm, paradigm, phlegm*

Likewise, the digraph *"gh"* is silent in numerous words. They are arranged by vowel sound preceding *"gh"*.

> /oʊ/ - *dough, though, although, borough, thorough*
>
> /aʊ/ - *bough, plough, sough, drought*
>
> /ɔː/ - *bought, brought, fought, thought, caught, naught, taught, daughter*
>
> /uː/ - *through, brougham*
>
> /eɪ/ - *straight, eight, neighbor, weigh, weight*
>
> /aɪ/ - *fight, high, knight, light, might, night, right, thigh, height, sleight*

In a similar fashion, the *"g"* works along with *"n"* in the digraph *"ng"* to form the /ŋ/ sound as in the examples below. The *"ng"* is frequently pronounced as /n/ instead of /ŋ/ in words with the suffix *"-ing"*; which is informally reflected in the spelling by omitting the "g". For example, the word *"singing"* is spelled as *"singin'"*. This is known as *"g-dropping"*, which is in reference to the spelling strictly, as there is no /g/ sound present in the standard /ŋ/.

> *cling, hang, long, lung, sing, coming, running, walking, willing, hanger, hangover, hanging, clingy, longing, singer, singing, willingly*

The *"x"* spelling features the phonetic sequence /gz/ in the following words.

> *Alexander, auxiliary, exact, exactly, exaggerate, exalt, exaltation, exam, examine, examination, example, exasperate, executive, exert, exist, existence, existential, exotic, exuberant, exude, exhaust, exhibit, exhilarate, exhort, exhume*

In parallel, *"x"* forms the /gʒ/ in these words.

> *luxury, luxurious*

Last but not least, it is useful to know about the phonological process known as devoicing; in which a normally voiced consonant is replaced by a voiceless one when adjacent to unvoiced sounds. This commonly happens when speaking fast. The words listed below could exhibit this phenomenon; with the voiced /g/ being devoiced to /k/.

> *beg for, bug killer, drug possession, drugstore, drug traffic, dogfood, eggshell*

Please, don't forget to record yourself saying the words, compare it to the model and make any necessary corrections. It is advisable to repeat this exercise on a daily basis. Furthermore, consider writing and practicing with tongue twisters and sentences that emphasize the pronunciation of /g/ in various topics and daily life scenarios.

Chapter 20

Minimal Pairs

k *and* g

The phonemes /k/ and /g/ are pronounced with the same mouth positions, but /k/ is articulated without engaging the vocal cords and with a greater release of air.

cab - gab	clamor - glamor	con - gone
caf - gaff	class - glass	coo - goo
came - game	clean - glean	core - gore
cane - gain	clue - glue	cosh - gosh
cap - gap	Co. - go	cot - got
cape - gape	coast - ghost	could - good
card - guard	coat - goat	coup - goo
cash - gash	cob - gob	course - gorse
cave - gave	cod - god	coy - goy
clad - glad	cold - gold	crab - grab
clam - glam	come - gum	cram - gram

cramps - gramps

crane - grain

crate - grate, great

craven - graven

craze - graze

crease - grease, Greece

creed - greed

creek - Greek

crepe - grape

crew - grew

crime - grime

cripes - gripes

croup - group

crow - grow

crowned - ground

crumble - grumble

cuff - guff

cull - gull

cunning - gunning

curd - gird

curly - girly

cut - gut

K - gay

kale - gale

key - ghee

kill - gill

kilt - gilt

kit - git

krill - grill

When /k/ or /g/ appear at the end of the word, they are difficult to differentiate. It can be useful to concentrate on releasing more air with /k/, as well as, to elongate the vowel before /g/ a little more than the one that comes before /k/.

back - bag

beck - beg

berk - berg

black - blag

block - blog

brick - brig

broke - brogue

buck - bug

chuck - chug

clock - clog

cock - cog

crack - crag

dick - dig

dock - dog

duck - dug

flock - flog

frock - frog

hack - hag

hock - hog

jack - jag

jock - jog

knack - nag   prick - prig   snack - snag

lack - lag   puck - pug   snuck - snug

leak - league   rack - rag   stack - stag

lock - log   ruck - rug   tack - tag

luck - lug   sack - sag   tuck - tug

muck - mug   shack - shag   whack - wag

pick - pig   slack - slag   wick - wig

pluck - plug   smock - smog

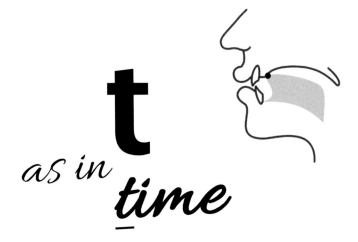

t

as in

time

T his phoneme represents the initial consonant sound in words such as *"time"* and *"take"*, the middle one in *"doctor"* and *"attack"*, and the final one in *"foot"* and *"cute"*. Its voiced counterpart is /d/.

This sound is described as an unvoiced alveolar plosive. The tip or blade of the tongue contacts the alveolar ridge and the airflow is blocked entirely in both the vocal and nasal tracts. You direct the airstream toward the center of the tongue and pressure it to the front, then you separate the tongue from the alveolar ridge, releasing the compressed air forward through the mouth only. It is produced without vibrations of the vocal cords.

This variant is also known as aspirated or true *"t"* since you have to puff air when you release the *"t"*. This one is always used at the beginning of words and is normally spelled *"t"*, but there are also some words using *"th"*.

> *"t"* - *tab, table, tag, tailor, take, tale, talent, talk, tall, tame, tan, tangle, tank, tap, tape, target, task, taste, tax, taxi, tea, teach, team, tease, technology, teeth, tell, ten, tend, tender, tennis, tense, tent, term, terror, test, text, tick, ticket, tide, tiger, tight, time, timid, tiny, tip, tire, tissue, titanic, titanium, tittle, today, together, toilet, tolerate, tongue, too, took, tool, top, topic, torch, toss, total, tough, tour, toward, town, toxic, toy, tub, tube, tuck, tumor, tune, tunnel, turbine, turkey, turn, turtle, tutor, tuxedo, tycoon, type, typhoon, typical, tyrant*
>
> *"th"* - **thyme, Thailand, Thames, Thomas**

In addition, the letter *"t"* and the digraph *"th"* are always pronounced with the true *"t"* in the middle of a word when it appears in a consonant cluster; not between vowels.

> *"t"* - *obtain, active, activity, actor, disinfectant, doctor, factor, reluctant, after, often, vegetable, altar, alter, altern, realtor, antibiotic, antibody, antidote, antihero, center, contact, contain, content, contingent, enter, entire, intact, interpreter, mantle, mental, mentality, scientist, onto, until, voluntary, baptize, chapter, empty, optic, advertise, articulate, cartoon, expertise, fertility, opportunity, particular, pertain, tortilla, transportation, astute, austere, booster, buster, cistern, costard, costume, cus-*

todian, customer, distant, dusty, hasty, instead, master, monster, nasty, pasta, pastor, piston, poster, pustule, rusty, sister, system, tasty, yesterday, stab, stable, staff, stage, stake, stall, stand, standard, star, state, static, stay, steal, steam, steel, stem, step, stick, stiff, still, stimulate, sting, stir, stitch, stock, stone, stood, stop, store, storm, story, stow, stubborn, stuck, study, stuff, stumble, stunt, style

"th" - apartheid, Anthony

You may also come across the aspirated "t" in the middle of a word between two vowels, but the "t" or "tt" must be at the beginning of a stressed syllable.

"t" - agitate, botanic, catastrophe, citation, detach, detail, detain, dietary, fatality, floatation, guitar, hesitate, Italian, imitate, imitation, invitation, irritate, limitation, meditate, metallic, military, monetary, mutation, notate, potassium, potato, quotation, reputation, retail, retain, retaliate, retard, rotate, sabotage, satanic, secretary, titanic, titanium, totality, vegetarian, antiterrorist, architecture, between, cafeteria, cemetery, criteria, deter, detect, detective, detention, determine, detest, eternal, intend, eighteen, hotel, material, maternity, motel, potential, pretend, protect, protest, strategic, utensil, appetite, autism, autistic, fatigue, maritime, petition, retina, retire, routine, statistics, utility, atomic, auditorium, autonomy, detour, dormitory, editorial, inflammatory, laboratory,

> *mandatory, notorious, oxytocin, rhetorical, territory, tu-torial, utopia, altitude, attitude, constitute, gratuity, lati-tude, longitude, magnitude, prostitute, return*
>
> *"tt" - attach, attack, attain, attempt, attend, attention, attorney, tattoo, attune*

By the same token, the true "t" may be present in more than one word together in normal speech. This may occur when a word ending in a consonant (excluding "r") + "t" is followed by a word starting with a vowel sound.

> *accept it, best of all, cost of, first of us, just a second, just in case, last of all, least amount, left out, lost in, most of people, next in line, taste in my mouth, trust it, waste of time, must'(ə)ve*

The /tr/ and /str/ clusters, due to assimilation, have been re-placed by the palato-alveolar consonant clusters /tʃr/ and /stʃr/ respectively. The following examples practice this pattern.

> /tʃr/ - **trace, track, trade, tradition, traffic, tragic, trail, trailer, train, trait, traitor, transfer, trap, trash, trauma, travel, tray, tread, treason, treat, tree, tremble, trend, trespass, triad, trial, triangle, tribe, tribune, trick, trig-ger, trip, triple, tripod, trim, triumph, trivia, troll, troop, tropical, trouble, trout, troy, truce, truck, true, truffle, trump, trumpet, trunk, trust, truth, try, tryptic, an**tr**ax, be**tr**ay, con**tr**act, con**tr**ary, con**tr**ast, en**tr**ance, illus**tr**ate, man**tr**a, neu**tr**al, orche**str**a, por**tr**ay, re**tr**act, ul**tr**a, ac-**

> tress, hatred, waitress, cartridge, centric, contribute, doctrine, electric, intrigue, intrinsic, patriot, retrieve, atrocity, control, introduce, metropolis, neutron, patrol, patron, retrospect, tightrope, altruist, intrude, intrusive, tantrum, spectrum, country, entry, pantry, poetry, poultry, retry, attribute, attract, buttress, mattress
>
> /stʃr/ - straight, strain, strand, strange, strap, strategy, straw, stray, stream, street, strength, stress, stretch, strict, stride, strike, string, strip, strive, stroke, stroll, strong, struck, structure, struggle, strung, abstract, astray, austral, distract, extra, lustral, extreme, mistreat, mistress, distribute, district, ostrich, restrict, astronaut, astronomy, destroy, construct, construe, destruct, extrude, instruct, instrument, mistrust, obstruct, chemistry, industry, ministry, pastry, registry

However, in General American when the "t" appears between vowels at the beginning of an unstressed syllable may get neutralized as /ɾ/. Then "butter" may be said /'bʌɾər/. This also happens between a vowel and the letter "l". It is interpreted by non-native English speakers as an "r" sound in many foreign languages.

This variant is described as an alveolar flap or tap. The tongue contacts the alveolar ridge lightly and releases immediately. The following words feature this sound spelled as "t" and "tt".

> "t" - avatar, beta, brutal, capital, capitalist, catalog, catalyst, catastrophic, cheetah, data, digital, fatal, footage, heritage, hospital, inevitable, metabolic, metaphor, met-

al, outage, petal, pivotal, profitable, suitable, total, vital, vitamin, cater, computer, daughter, diameter, gataway, gluteus, heater, item, latency, later, lateral, latex, literal, meter, meteor, noted, outer, parameter, perimeter, reiterate, router, satellite, scooter, uterus, veteran, veterinary, water, citizen, critic, cutie, dramatic, executive, fetish, marketing, motive, negative, notice, notify, pathetic, poetic, political, positive, rating, relative, scrutiny, static, satisfy, anatomy, atom, auditor, autograph, autopsy, calculator, clitoris, creator, editor, elevator, gator, indicator, janitor, monitor, monotony, motor, operator, photo, potato, protocol, prototype, rhetoric, senator, tomato, tutor, visitor, apparatus, autumn, fetus, hiatus, scrutum, setup, sputum, status, stratum, city, facility, pity, security, utility, subtle, title

"tt" - cottage, vendetta, batter, better, bitter, clutter, flatter, glitter, letter, litter, matter, otter, pattern, potter, shatter, shutter, utter, attic, attitude, bottom, buttock, button, falsetto, motto, risotto, lettuce, petty, pretty, battle, bottle, cattle, little, rattle, settle, throttle

This rule also includes the final "t" when adding suffixes like "-er", "-est", "-ed", "-ing" and "-y".

fighter, lighter, visitor, waiter, writer, greater, hotter, greatest, hottest, fitted, lighted, limited, matted, sighted, united, waited, exciting, fighting, greeting, inviting, meeting, visiting, waiting, writing, chatty, shitty

Moreover, the flapped "t" also occurs when "t" is between an "r" and a vowel at the beginning of an unstressed syllable.

> article, artificial, artist, certify, charter, courtesy, courteous, dirty, fertile, flirty, fortify, forty, liberty, mortal, mortified, party, property, poverty, puberty, quarter, starter, thirty, turtle, vertical, vertigo, vortex, comforter, converter, reporter, supporter, shorter, smarter, shortest, smartest, adverted, alerted, assorted, deported, distorted, escorted, exported, farted, flirted, introverted, reported, sorted, started, comforting, hurting, supporting, assertive, supportive

In the same fashion, this phenomenon can be encountered in phrases when a word ending in vowel + "t" or vowel + "rt" is followed by a word starting with a vowel sound.

> about it, a lot of, at a time, beat up, brought it up, caught up, cut off, cut out, date it, eat it, edit it, great at, figure it out, get along, get away, get over, get out, it all, it isn't, let it out, let us, not at all, out of, put away, put it off, put it out, right out, set up, spit it out, split up, straight up, thought out, wait a minute, what about, what a surprise, what if, write up, airport on, expert in, part of, report it, start in, sort of, might'(ə)ve

Similarly, if a word ends in vowel, vowel + "r", or vowel + "t" or "d", the following word starting with "t" may be pronounced as a flapped "t".

> *easy to say, forty to fifty, how to play, ready to go, say to*
> *you, way to go, see you tomorrow, quarter to five, about*
> *to go, needed to go, wanted to go*

On the other hand, there are a number of words with a "t" + unstressed vowel + "n", in which the "t" is pronounced as a glottal stop /ʔ/ like in "uh-oh". This one is made when the airflow through your mouth is stopped by either your tongue or lips, causing a build-up of air that is released through the mouth causing a small, explosive sound.

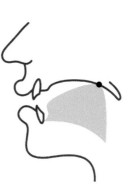

> *certain, curtain, fountain, mountain, plantain, accoun-*
> *tant, assistant, blatant, combatant, constant, hesitant,*
> *important, instant, irritant, militant, mutant, pollutant,*
> *beaten, bitten, eaten, enlighten, flatten, forgotten, fright-*
> *en, gluten, kindergarten, kitten, lighten, mitten, shorten,*
> *smitten, straighten, sweeten, tighten, threaten, written,*
> *sentence, competency, competent, consistent, inter-*
> *mittent, patent, persistent, remittent, latin, badminton,*
> *button, carton, cotton, glutton, molten, rotten, skele-*
> *ton, triton, Manhattan, Burton, Clinton, Hilton, Newton,*
> *might(ə)n't*

Sometimes the /t/ sound disappears entirely. This often happens when the "t" comes right after "n" and the speaker is talking quickly.

> *county, dentist, entity, into, panty, plenty, twenty, Santa,*

> *Toronto, gentle, gentleman, mantle, advantage, percent-age, continent, sentiment, sentinel, accounting, disappointing, fainting, presenting, complimentary, documentary, dented, painted, pointed, printed, wanted, center, painter, printer, splinter, winter, counter, counteract, counterattack, counterfeit, identification, identify, identical, identity, enterprise, entertain, interact, intercept, interface, interfere, international, Internet, intersection, interrupt, interval, intervene, interview, accidental, coincidental, continental, dental, fundamental, mental, rental, sentimental, argumentative, representative*

This also happens with contiguous words in a phrase.

> *amount of, different address, in front of, point out, print out, present at, went out, must(ə)n't, listen to me, seven to ten, ten to six*

Furthermore, there are multiple examples exhibiting a silent "t" in English, many of which have the endings "-stle", "-sten" and less frequently "-ften".

> *apostle, bristle, bustle, castle, gristle, hustle, nestle, pestle, rustle, thistle, whistle, wrestle, Mistletoe, chasten, christen, fasten, glisten, hasten, listen, moisten, often, soften*

Equivalently, some other words are just pronounced with a silent "t" by most native speakers; most of which are loanwords from French.

> chestnut, Christmas, mortgage, ballet, bouquet, buffet, cabaret, cachet, chalet, gourmet, ricochet, tourniquet, valet, debut, depot, rapport

On the flip side, at the end of words, Americans often use a stopped "t", which is referred to as a held "t" as the mouth is shaped as though to form the true /t/ sound, but simply stop the airflow with the tongue at the ridge behind the teeth rather than releasing it to articulate the sound. You can find this held "t" spelled as "t" and "tt", both with a representation of magic "e".

> "t" - about, at, beat, but, chat, credit, cut, eat, eight, feet, fight, fit, flat, format, get, great, hit, hot, it, let, light, lot, market, meet, met, net, night, not, out, put, set, spirit, split, street, that, threat, treat, unit, visit, wet, what, act, fact, exact, extract, impact, left, adult, bolt, colt, molt, result, volt, agent, amount, client, current, different, front, government, moment, parent, plant, point, present, recent, sent, want, went, except, script, art, effort, heart, part, report, short, smart, sort, sport, start, august, best, coast, cost, east, first, just, last, least, lost, most, must, past, west, next
>
> "t" + Magic "e" - create, date, debate, donate, fate, gate, hate, late, mate, pirate, plate, rate, relate, skate, slate, state, athlete, compete, complete, concrete, delete, discrete, appetite, bite, cite, despite, excite, ignite, infinite, invite, kite, lite, polite, quite, site, smite, white, write, anecdote, antidote, denote, devote, note, promote,

quote, remote, vote, absolute, acute, brute, cute, dispute, flute, lute, minute, mute, route, salute, suite, byte, forte, chaste, haste, paste, taste, waste

"tt" - boycott, butt, matt, mutt, watt

"tt" + Magic "e" - briquette, brunette, cassette, cigarette, courgette, etiquette, gazette, latte, marionette, matte, palette, pirouette, rosette, roulette, serviette, silhouette

Same happens when the "t" appears before a consonant sound in the middle of words, mostly derivative and compound words. The "t" is pronounced as a held "t".

antler, atmosphere, bitcoin, butler, cutlery, outlet, platinum, network, outside, partner, postcard, postman, postpone, utmost, brightness, fitness, lightness, witness, countless, dauntless, pointless, relentless, adjustment, appointment, commitment, department, disappointment, ointment, treatment, fortunately, immediately, infinitely, intimately, privately, separately, ultimately

In the same way, the suffix "-ed" in the past tense of regular verbs is pronounced as a held "t" when the last letter of the verb is a voiceless consonant.

/p/ - dropped, equipped, flipped, grasped, helped, jumped, kidnapped, popped, reaped, skipped, stopped, trapped, tripped, whipped, zipped

106

/k/ - ask**ed**, link**ed**, mark**ed**, park**ed**, rank**ed**, smirk**ed**, stalk**ed**, talk**ed**, thank**ed**, walk**ed**, work**ed**, wreak**ed**, lock**ed**, nick**ed**, pick**ed**, track**ed**, trick**ed**, frolick**ed**, mim-ick**ed**, panick**ed**, picnick**ed**

/f/ - barf**ed**, bluff**ed**, cough**ed**, laugh**ed**, sniff**ed**, surf**ed**

/θ/ - froth**ed**

/s/ - access**ed**, cross**ed**, foss**ed**, guess**ed**, impuls**ed**, kiss**ed**, mess**ed**, miss**ed**, pass**ed**, promis**ed**, releas**ed**, stress**ed**

/ʃ/ - brush**ed**, cherish**ed**, clash**ed**, crash**ed**, demolish**ed**, distinguish**ed**, finish**ed**, polish**ed**, punish**ed**, push**ed**, rush**ed**, smash**ed**, splash**ed**, vanish**ed**, wash**ed**, wish**ed**

/tʃ/ - approach**ed**, attach**ed**, ditch**ed**, fetch**ed**, itch**ed**, launch**ed**, match**ed**, patch**ed**, pitch**ed**, reach**ed**, re-proach**ed**, search**ed**, stitch**ed**, stretch**ed**, touch**ed**, watch**ed**, wrench**ed**, vouch**ed**

It is noteworthy that when speaking fast in informal questions with a *"you"* subject, the /j/ is often blended into the final sound of the previous word when ending with /t/. Therefore, the unstressed sequence /tj/ coalesces into an affricate sound /tʃ/.

/tʃ/ - wha**t y**ou doing? (wha**tch**a doin'?), won'**t y**ou go? (won'**tch**a go?), ain'**t y**ou come? (ain'**tch**a come?), don't

107

you hear? (don'tcha hear?), didn't you see? (didn'cha see?), bet you! (betcha!), got you! (gotcha!)

Last but not least, the letter "t" is next to silent letters in the words below.

victual, yacht, bought, thought, light, fight, debt, doubt, subtle

Please, don't forget to record yourself saying the words, compare it to the model and make any necessary corrections. It is advisable to repeat this exercise on a daily basis. Furthermore, consider writing and practicing with tongue twisters and sentences that emphasize the pronunciation of /t/ in various topics and daily life scenarios.

d

as in *day*

This phoneme represents the initial consonant sound in words such as *"dog"* and *"drink"*, and the final one in *"food"* and *"hide"*. For Spanish speakers the main difficulty is the difference between /d/ and /ð/. Its unvoiced counterpart is /t/.

This sound is described as a voiced alveolar plosive. The tip or blade of the tongue contacts the alveolar ridge and the airflow is blocked entirely in both the vocal and nasal tracts. You direct the airstream toward the center of the tongue and pressure it to the front, then you separate the tongue from the alveolar ridge, releasing the compressed air forward through the mouth only. The aspiration for /d/ is less than the one for /t/. Vibrate your vocal cords as you make this sound.

This variant is also known as true *"d"*. It is always used at the beginning of words and normally spelled *"d"*.

dad, dairy, daisy, dam, damage, damn, damp, dance, danger, dark, dart, dash, data, date, dawn, day, dazzle, dead, deaf, deal, dear, debt, debut, decide, deep, deer, define, delay, delicate, demand, demo, den, design, desk, develop, devil, diamond, diaper, diary, dice, die, diet, differ, different, digit, dinner, dinosaur, direct, disc, disease, dish, disk, ditch, dive, divide, divorce, doctor, dodge, dog, doll, dollar, dolphin, domino, done, donut, doom, dose, dot, doubt, dove, down, dozen, dual, duck, ductile, due, duke, dull, dumb, dump, dungeon, duplicate, during, dust, duty, dye

In addition, the letter "*d*" is always pronounced with the true "*d*" in the middle of a word when it appears in a consonant cluster; not between vowels.

abdomen, anecdote, boulder, building, bulldozer, folder, golden, holder, mildew, moldy, seldom, shoulder, welder, update, updo, jeopardize, ordeal, ordinary, overdue, sardine, disdain, wisdom, countdown, letdown, outdate, outdoor, shutdown, agenda, boundary, calendar, foundation, mandatory, panda, sandal, scandal, standard, Sunday, endeavor, gender, indeed, index, pandemic, reminder, render, slender, tendency, tender, thunder, under, wonder, candidate, condition, handicap, indicate, individual, pending, splendid, abandon, condom, indoor, kingdom, random, rundown, undo, window, conduct, endure, indulge, industry, roundup, undue, bundle, candle, dwindle, handle, swindle

You can also find the true *"d"* in the middle of a word between two vowels, but the *"d"* or *"dd"* must be at the beginning of a stressed syllable.

> *"d"* - adapt, adapter, affidavit, audacity, candidate, consolidate, degradation, didactic, dromedary, intimidate, macadamia, medallion, modality, oxidation, pedantic, predate, redact, sedate, sedation, solidarity, solidary, today, validate, academic, accidental, bodega, citadel, coincidental, confidential, credential, duodenum, edema, fidelity, idea, identical, identify, identity, incidental, pedestrian, presidential, prudential, psychedelic, redeem, redemption, residential, vedette, audition, contradict, crocodile, edition, judicial, medieval, nadir, nudism, paradigm, paradise, periodicity, prediction, ridiculous, tradition, adobe, adopt, adorable, adore, adorn, antidote, idolatry, orthodox, paradox, pseudonym, voodoo, adult, adultery, deduce, deduct, introduce, produce, reduce, redundant, seduce, seductive, traduce
>
> *"dd"* - addict, addiction, addictive, addition, adduce, adduct, adduction, adductor

Similarly, the true *"d"* may be present in more than one word together in normal speech. This may occur when a word ending in a consonant (excluding *"r"*) + *"d"* is followed by a word starting with a vowel sound.

> band aid, behind of, find out, fond of, kind of, send out, sold out, stand out, stand up, wind up

On a few occasions the digraph *"dd"* is pronounced as two separate /d/, which is represented as /d.d/.

*go**dd**amn, hea**dd**ress, mi**dd**ay, upsi**d**e-**d**own*

Due to assimilation, the /dr/ cluster has been replaced by the palato-alveolar consonant cluster /dʒr/. The following examples practice this pattern.

Initial Position - **dr**aft, **dr**ag, **dr**agon, **dr**ain, **dr**ake, **dr**ama, **dr**apery, **dr**astic, **dr**aught, **dr**aw, **dr**awer, **dr**ead, **dr**eam, **dr**ess, **dr**ew, **dr**ibble, **dr**ift, **dr**ill, **dr**ink, **dr**ip, **dr**ive, **dr**izzle, **dr**one, **dr**op, **dr**ought, **dr**ove, **dr**own, **dr**owsy, **dr**udge, **dr**ug, **dr**um, **dr**ummer, **dr**unk, **dr**y

Middle Position - *cathe**dr**al, hy**dr**ate, melo**dr**ama, quad-rant, tun**dr**a, with**dr**aw, a**dr**enaline, chil**dr**en, hun**dr**ed, scoun**dr**el, cylin**dr**ical, hy**dr**ic, man**dr**ill, qua**dr**iceps, ten-**dr**ill, an**dr**oid, an**dr**ogen, caul**dr**on, hy**dr**ogen, rain**dr**op, squa**dr**on, syn**dr**ome, war**dr**obe, won**dr**ous, anti**dr**ug, ear**dr**um, qua**dr**uple, foun**dr**y, laun**dr**y, sun**dr**y, a**dd**ress*

However, in General American when the *"d"* appears between vowels at the beginning of an unstressed syllable may get neutralized as /ɾ/. Then *"la**dd**er"* may be said /'læɾər/. This also happens between a vowel and the letter *"l"*. It is interpreted by non-native English speakers as an *"r"* sound in many foreign languages.

This variant is described as an alveolar flap or tap. The tongue contacts the alveolar ridge lightly and releases immediately. The following words present this sound spelled as *"d"* and *"dd"*.

> *"d"* - *avoidance, bridal, feudal, guidance, headache, madam, medal, modal, nowadays, pedal, pedant, predator, radar, soda, suicidal, tidal, academy, adequate, antecedent, broaden, cadence, consider, federal, hideous, leader, maiden, model, modern, modest, pedestal, predecessor, president, prudent, evident, reader, rodent, rodeo, sided, slider, student, trader, video, widen, wooden, audible, audio, audit, credible, credit, dedicate, edible, edit, gladiator, gradient, idiom, idiot, immediate, incredible, ingredient, insidious, ludicrous, media, medicine, modify, meditate, medium, meridian, obedient, podium, prejudice, radial, radiant, radio, radius, radish, ridicule, stadium, studio, zodiac, adolescent, avocado, corridor, freedom, idol, kudos, meadow, odor, odorant, shadow, torpedo, tradeoff, tuxedo, widow, product, already, body, comedy, greedy, lady, melody, ready, steady, study, tidy, cradle, doodle, ladle, needle, noodle, poodle*
>
> *"dd"* - *cheddar, riddance, bladder, forbidden, goddess, hidden, ladder, odder, shredder, shudder, sudden, oddity, reddish, wedding, kiddo, paddock, cuddle, fiddle, middle, muddle, paddle, puddle, riddle*

This rule also encompasses the final *"d"* when adding suffixes like *"-er"*, *"-est"*, *"-ed"*, *"-ing"* and *"-y"*.

> *louder, sadder, loudest, saddest, headed, needed, loaded, bedding, feeding, reading, riding, bloody, needy*

113

Moreover, the flapped "*d*" is also featured when "*d*" is between an "*r*" and a vowel at the beginning of an unstressed syllable.

> *accordant, affordable, verdant, ardent, awarded, border, burden, guarded, garden, harden, murder, order, recorded, stewardess, according, cardiac, cardio, cardigan, cardinal, coordinate, guardian, hoarding, ordinal, ordinary, regarding, rewarding, sordid, verdict, ardor, boredom, cordon, hairdom, hazardous, pardon, stardom, weirdo, perdurable, hardy, jeopardy, sturdy, tardy, wordy, curdle, girdle, hurdle*

In a similar fashion, this phenomenon can be encountered in phrases when a word ending in vowel + "*d*", or vowel + "*rd*" is followed by a word starting with a vowel sound.

> *add on, excited about, fraud alert, method of, wanted it, I don't know, could'(ə)ve, should'(ə)ve, would'(ə)ve*

On the other hand, in the following words "*d*" is pronounced as a glottal stop /ʔ/ like in "*uh-oh*". This one is made when the airflow is stopped, causing a build-up of air that when released causes a short, explosive sound.

> *did(ə)n't, had(ə)n't, could(ə)n't, should(ə)n't, would(ə)n't*

Conversely, some other words are just said with a silent "*d*".

> *handsome, handkerchief, sandwich, Wednesday*

On the flip side, at the end of words, Americans often stop the /d/ before releasing the build-up air, which is referred to as a held "d". The mouth is shaped as though to form the true /d/ sound and the tongue touches the alveolar ridge, but doesn't release the airflow. It is like you never finish making the sound. It is found as "d", "dd" and also magic "e".

"d" - aid, bad, bed, bid, blood, dad, dead, did, feed, food, fraud, glad, god, good, grid, had, head, kid, lead, led, lid, load, loud, mad, method, mood, mud, need, pad, read, red, rid, road, sad, wood, bold, build, child, cold, field, fold, gold, hold, mild, old, sold, told, wild, world, and, band, behind, bond, demand, end, expand, find, found, friend, fund, ground, hand, island, kind, land, lend, mind, pond, round, sand, second, send, sound, spend, stand, tend, wind, award, awkward, bird, board, card, ford, hard, lord, third, ward, word

"d" + Magic "e" - bade, ballade, blade, blockade, brigade, cascade, facade, fade, glade, grade, jade, lemonade, made, parade, persuade, promenade, shade, spade, trade, accede, cede, concede, impede, precede, stampede, bride, decide, guide, hide, pride, provide, reside, ride, side, slide, suicide, tide, wide, code, electrode, episode, explode, implode, mode, attitude, crude, dude, elude, exclude, gratitude, include, magnitude, nude, prelude, rude, horde

"dd" - add, odd

Same happens when the "d" appears before a consonant sound in the middle of a word, in most cases by making compound words or adding a suffix.

> administrate, admire, admit, admission, advance, advantage, adventure, advertise, advise, advocate, bedbug, bedsheet, bloodstream, broadcast, cardboard, deadline, feedback, fundraiser, grandmother, grandson, goldfish, goodbye, handcuff, handbag, handmade, headline, headmaster, headquarter, headset, hindsight, kidnap, kidney, landlord, landmark, landscape, medley, midnight, mindblown, mindset, padlock, roadside, roundtable, roundtrip, sidebar, sideburns, sidecar, sideline, soundtrack, standby, standpoint, standstill, toddler, trademark, treadmill, wildfire, childhood, friendship, dreadful, handful, mindfull, fondness, goodness, kindness, oddness, madness, redness, boundless, endless, mindless, needless, regardless, amendment, oddment, badly, friendly, hardly, kindly, oddly, repeatedly, thirdly

In the same way, the suffix "-ed" in the past tense of regular verbs is pronounced as /d/ when the last letter of the verb is a voiced consonant or vowel sound.

> /b/ - absorbed, described, disturbed, grabbed, perturbed, rubbed, scrubbed, sobbed, stabbed
>
> /g/ - begged, dragged, drugged, jogged, logged, plugged, tagged

/v/ - arriv**ed**, behav**ed**, carv**ed**, evolv**ed**, liv**ed**, lov**ed**, pav**ed**, sav**ed**, solv**ed**, wav**ed**, weav**ed**

/ð/ - bath**ed**, breath**ed**, cloth**ed**, loath**ed**, mouth**ed**, sooth**ed**, swath**ed**

/z/ - buzz**ed**, caus**ed**, compos**ed**, compris**ed**, eras**ed**, expos**ed**, fizz**ed**, paus**ed**, prais**ed**, quizz**ed**, rais**ed**, us**ed**

/dʒ/ - ag**ed**, aveng**ed**, barg**ed**, chang**ed**, charg**ed**, dodg**ed**, engag**ed**, hing**ed**, judg**ed**, urg**ed**, wag**ed**

/l/ - boil**ed**, dial**ed**, drill**ed**, expell**ed**, fulfill**ed**, label**ed**, re-veal**ed**, spell**ed**, thrill**ed**, yell**ed**

/r/ - answer**ed**, car**ed**, enter**ed**, fear**ed**, offer**ed**, pour**ed**, referr**ed**, scar**ed**, spurr**ed**, stirr**ed**, water**ed**

/m/ - bloom**ed**, calm**ed**, climb**ed**, dimm**ed**, film**ed**, harm**ed**, scamm**ed**, warm**ed**

/n/ - abandon**ed**, bann**ed**, chain**ed**, clean**ed**, concern**ed**, design**ed**, earn**ed**, sign**ed**

/ŋ/ - bang**ed**, belong**ed**, hang**ed**, long**ed**, prolong**ed**

Vowels - free**d**, pee**d**, marri**ed**, studi**ed**, worri**ed**, ski**ed**, crow**ed**, flow**ed**, glow**ed**, allow**ed**, bow**ed**, vow**ed**, de-

> layed, played, stayed, cried, fried, tried, dyed, died, lied, tied, annoyed, destroyed, enjoyed

Furthermore, the "-ed" adds an extra syllable pronounced as /ɪd/, when the regular verbs end either with /t/ or /d/ sounds.

> /t/ - committed, limited, united, visited, wanted

> /d/ - added, decided, ended, folded, needed

In the following exemptions, "-ed" is pronounced /ɪd/, despite not ending in /t/ or /d/.

> aged, alleged, beloved, blessed, crooked, dogged, legged, naked, ragged, wicked, wretched

It is noteworthy that when speaking fast in informal questions with a "you" subject, the /j/ is often blended into the final sound of the previous word when it ends with /d/. Therefore, the unstressed sequence /dj/ coalesces into an affricate sound /dʒ/.

> /dʒ/ - did you go? (didja go?), could you come? (couldja come?), would you stop? (wouldja stop?)

The letter "d" is next to silent letters in the words below.

> solder, could, should, would

Lastly, it is useful to know about the phonological process known as devoicing; in which a normally voiced consonant is replaced by a voiceless one when adjacent to unvoiced sounds. This commonly happens when speaking fast. The words listed below could exhibit this phenomenon; with the voiced /d/ sound being devoiced to /t/.

> *bad time, blood test, broadcast, cold place, disdain, gold frame, good songs, handcuff, headquarter, lead character, loud people, mild smell, old face, red carpet, roundtrip, sidetrack, standpoint*

Please, don't forget to record yourself saying the words, compare it to the model and make any necessary corrections. It is advisable to repeat this exercise on a daily basis. Furthermore, consider writing and practicing with tongue twisters and sentences that emphasize the pronunciation of /d/ in various topics and daily life scenarios.

Chapter 23

Minimal Pairs

t *and* d

In general terms, the initial /t/ and /d/ sounds are more readily distinguishable compared to their final counterparts. While the mouth and tongue configurations are quite similar, the production of /t/ involves the release of a greater amount of air without the use of vocal cords, at times making it almost like spitting. This airflow can be felt on the hand if held in front of the mouth.

tab - dab	tear - dare	tick - dick
tail, tale - dale	tear - dear	tide - died, dyed
tame - dame	tech - deck	tie - die, dye
tamp - damp	teed - deed	tier - deer
tank - dank	teen - dean	till - dill
tart - dart	tell - dell	tin - din
teal - deal	ten - den	tine - dine
team - deem	tent - dent	tint - dint

tip - dip	too - do	try - dry
tire - dire	toss - doss	tub - dub
titch - ditch	tote - dote	tuck - duck
toast - dosed	touch - Dutch	tug - dug
tock - dock	tough - duff	tummy - dummy
toe - doe	tout - doubt	tusk - dusk
toes - doze	tower - dour	tux - ducks
tomb - doom	town - down	two - do
ton - done	train - drain	tyke - dike
tongue - dung	tresses - dresses	tyre - dire

When /t/ or /d/ appear at the end of the word, they are often held. This makes the differentiation between these two sounds somewhat difficult. A useful tip is to elongate the vowel before /d/ a little more than the one that comes before /t/.

ant - and	cot - cod	grit - grid
at - add	cute - queued	hat - had
bat - bad	debt - dead	heart - hard
beat - bead	eight - aid	heat - heed
bent - bend	faint - feigned	height - hide
bet - bed	fat - fad	hit - hid
bleat - bleed	fate - fade	hot - hod
blurt - blurred	feet - feed	hurt - heard
bright - bride	float - flowed	it - id
but - bud	font - fond	kit - kid
cart - card	gloat - glowed	mat - mad
cat - cad	goat - goad	meant - mend
clot - clod	got - god	meet - mead

moat - mode	short - shored
mount - mound	shunt - shunned
neat - need	sight - side
not - nod	site - sighed
nought - gnawed	skint - skinned
oat - owed	skit - skid
pant - panned	slight - slide
pat - pad	slit - slid
peat - peed	sought - sawed
pert - purred	spent - spend
plaint - planed	spite - spied
plate - played	spurt - spurred
pleat - plead	state - stayed
plot - plod	stoat - stowed
port - poured	stunt - stunned
pot - pod	tart - tarred
punt - punned	teat - teed
quit - quid	tent - tend
route - rude	tight - tied
sat - sad	tint - tinned
scant - scanned	trot - trod
sent - send	wait - weighed
set - said	write - ride
sheet - she'd	

Chapter 24

Minimal Pairs

t *and* tʃ

The pronunciation of /t/ involves placing the tongue on the top of the mouth just behind the teeth and pulling it down, creating a disapproving *"tut tut"* sound. On the other hand, /tʃ/ is pronounced without tongue movement and with more air released, similar to a sneeze that is capable of moving a piece of paper or felt on the hand. It is similar to /dʒ/ but without the voice and with more air released.

art - arch	*bleat - bleach*
bat - batch	*blot - blotch*
beat, beet - beach, beech	*bot - botch*
belt - belch	*cat - catch*
bent - bench	*catty - catchy*
bit - bitch	*coat - coach*
bitty - bitchy	*eat - each*

flint - flinch	port - porch	till - chill
hat - hatch	pout - pouch	time - chime
hit - hitch	punt - punch	tin - chin
hoot - hooch	rent - wrench	tip - chip
hunt - hunch	rote, wrote - roach	tit - chit
hut - hutch	Scot - Scotch	toes - chose
it - itch	start - starch	toke - choke
lint - lynch	tap - chap	too, two - chew
mart - march	tar - char	top - chop
mat - match	tart - chart	tore - chore
moot - mooch	tat - chat	tubby - chubby
mutt - much	teak - cheek	tug - chug
not - notch	tear - chair	turn - churn
out - ouch	tear - cheer	turps - chirps
part - parch	tease - cheese	tut - touch
pat - patch	test - chest	twit - twitch
peat - peach	tick - chick	twos - choose
pert - perch	tide - chide	what - watch
pit - pitch	tiled - child	wit - which, witch

Chapter 25

Minimal Pairs

d *and* dʒ

The phoneme /dʒ/ is a voiced affricate produced with a significant release of air from a rounded mouth shape. Similarly, /d/ is a voiced stop sound where the tongue is positioned behind the top teeth.

bad - badge	dear - jeer	dive - jive
barred - barge	debt - jet	do - Jew
bud - budge	deep - jeep	dob - job
charred - charge	dell - gel	dock - jock
dab - jab	dig - jig	dog - jog
dale - jail	dim - gym	dosh - josh
dam, damn - jam	din - gin	doss - joss
dangle - jangle	dink - jink	dot - jot
day - J, jay	dinks - jinx	doused - joust
deans - jeans	dissed - gist	dread - dredge

D's - geez   head - hedge   rid - ridge
dug - jug   led - ledge   seed - siege
dump - jump   mid - midge   sled - sledge
dunk - junk   paid - page   wed - wedge
dust - just   pled - pledge   weighed - wage
ford - forge   purred - purge
gored - gorge   raid - rage

p
as in **put**

This phoneme represents the initial consonant sound in words such as *"push"* and *"place"*, and the final one in *"ship"*, *"stop"* and *"type"*. Its voiced counterpart is /b/.

This sound is described as an unvoiced bilabial plosive. You squeeze your lips together and block the airflow entirely in both the vocal and nasal tracts. Then, build up air against the closure while briefly holding the lips back before releasing the air with a small puff. This sound is produced without any vibrations of the vocal cords.

The spelling of this phoneme is very straightforward. The letter *"p"* reliably evokes /p/ in the different positions within a word.

Initial Position - ***part, passion, pattern, patient, pause, peace, peak, people, perfect, persuade, pick, picture,*** *pillow, pilot, pocket, polite, poor, position, public, puppy, purchase, put, push, pyramid, pyro, python, place, planet, plant, plastic, plea, please, plenty, plier, plight, plot, plough, ploy, plug, plumber, plural, plus, practice, praise, prank, pray, present, press, prey, price, princess, prison, privilege, problem, profit, project, prove, prudent*

Middle Position - *company, despair, expand, surpass, cooper, expect, opera, hospital, opinion, typical, empower, report, transport, vapor, octopus, popular, repulse, reputation, crispy, occupy, space, span, spark, specific, speed, spell, spend, spin, spirit, spit, spoil, spoon, sport, spot, spur, spy, splash, split, spray, spread, spring, spruce, display, explain, replay, complement, perplex, couple, example, multiple, people, sample, simple, staple, triple, explicit, deploy, explore, implore, surplus, deprave, soprano, express, impress, interpret, supreme, surprise, apron, improve, clipboard, soapbox, humpback, upbeat, cupcake, popcorn, update, updraft, campfire, helpful, upgrade, uphold, napkin, pumpkin, equipment, topmost, hypnotize, adapt, adopt, apt, empty, optic, slept*

Final Position - *cap, cheap, crap, gap, leap, map, nap, rap, reap, snap, soap, swap, tap, trap, wrap, deep, jeep, keep, rep, sheep, sleep, steep, step, sweep, chip, clip, dip, drip, flip, grip, hip, lip, ship, skip, slip, strip, tip, trip, whip, zip, bop, chop, cop, crap, crop, develop, drop, flop, gallop, hop, loop, mop, pop, shop, snoop, stop, top, backup, cup, group, hiccup, setup, soup, syrup, help, pulp, burp,* harp, sharp, usurp, bump, camp, damp, dump, jump, lamp, lump, pump, ramp, shrimp, stamp, swamp, tramp

Additionally, you can find multiple words presenting the letter "p" and magic "e".

grape, rape, scape, shape, tape, crepe, pipe, ripe, snipe, stripe, swipe, tripe, wipe, cope, dope, hope, rope, scope, slope, trope, coupe, troupe, hype, type, Thorpe

Likewise, the spelling "pp" can be observed as follows.

Middle Position - appall, apparel, apparent, stoppage, appeal, appear, appease, appendicitis, copper, happen, pepper, puppet, supper, upper, zipper, hippie, appoint, opponent, opportunity, oppose, opposite, support, suppose, suppurate, floppy, happy, puppy, applause, appliance, apply, supplement, supply, apple, cripple, nipple, ripple, scrapple, appraise, appreciate, apprehend, apprise, approach, approve, oppress, suppress

Final Position - app

Magic "e" - shoppe

On the other hand, the "p" is exceptionally silent in the following words.

coup, receipt, cupboard, raspberry, corps, pneumonia, psalm, pseudo, pseudonym, psoriasis, psych, psychic,

> *psychology, psychiatry, psychiatrist, psychotherapy, psychedelic, psychopath, psychotic*

It is beneficial to know about the phonological process known as voicing or sonorization; in which a normally voiceless consonant becomes voiced when adjacent to voiced sounds. It tends to be more common when speaking fast. The words listed below often exhibit this phenomenon; with the voiceless /p/ being voiced to /b/.

> *cheap dress, clipboard, deep water, drop back, gap year, humpback, leap year, pop music, sleep there, soapbox, stop by, tap water, top-notch, trapdoor, upbeat, update, upgrade*

Please, don't forget to record yourself saying the words, compare it to the model and make any necessary corrections. It is advisable to repeat this exercise on a daily basis. Furthermore, consider writing and practicing with tongue twisters and sentences that emphasize the pronunciation of /p/ in various topics and daily life scenarios.

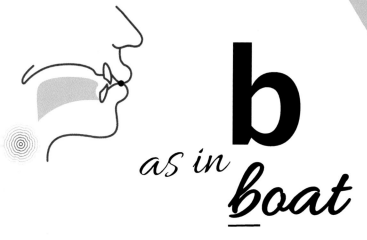

as in

b

boat

This phoneme represents the initial consonant sound in words such as *"bed"* and *"black"*, and the final one in *"club"*, *"verb"* and *"globe"*. Its unvoiced counterpart is /p/.

This sound is described as an unvoiced bilabial plosive. You close your lips and block the airflow entirely in both the vocal and nasal tracts. Then, push air through the mouth against the closure while briefly holding the lips back before releasing the air with a small puff. Vibrate your vocal cords during the articulation.

/b/ is typically represented by the letter *"b"* in most cases.

Initial Position - *bacon, ball, banner, baptize, bargain, battle, bear, bed, begin, behavior, below, benefit, billboard, biology, bird, birthday, bitter, board, body, book, bottom,*

131

bound, boy, build, bull, burden, busy, butter, button, by, bypass, byte, black, bladder, blame, bland, bleak, bleed, blend, bless, blind, bliss, blister, blizzard, block, blog, blood, blow, blue, bluff, blunt, blur, brag, brain, brand, brave, bread, break, breath, breed, brick, brief, bring, brittle, broad, brook, brother, brow, bruise, brunch, brunette, brush, brutal, brute

Middle Position - combat, debate, embassy, husband, chamber, iceberg, maybe, number, obesity, remember, cabin, cubic, forbid, habit, about, bamboo, carbon, harbor, rainbow, robot, abuse, debut, omnibus, suburb, tribute, vocabulary, abysm, baby, lullaby, nearby, problem, tablespoon, able, audible, available, cable, capable, double, enable, noble, possible, stable, table, trouble, vegetable, visible, goblin, oblige, oblivion, public, publish, celebrate, embrace, library, vibrate, jailbreak, umbrella, debris, fabric, hybrid, rubric, abroad, embroider, abrupt, subgroup, subject, sublime, submit, subsist, substance, subtitle, subtle, subvert, subway, bobcat, abdomen, abduct, abnegate, abnormal, obnoxious, webpage, absent, obsess, absorb, absurd, website, obtain, obvious

Final Position - cab, crab, grab, lab, rehab, slab, stab, tab, web, crib, rib, cob, job, knob, mob, rob, snob, sob, throb, club, cub, hub, pub, rub, scrub, shrub, snub, tub, alb, bulb, barb, carb, adverb, herb, proverb, superb, verb, absorb, orb, curb, disturb, perturb, suburb

Same happens with *"b"* + magic *"e"* in the words below.

> *babe, bribe, describe, inscribe, subscribe, tribe, vibe, anaerobe, bathrobe, earlobe, globe, lobe, microbe, probe, robe, strobe, wardrobe, xenophobe, zoophobe, cube, lube, tube*

Besides, the digraph *"bb"* is another representation.

> Middle Position - *cabbage, clubber, robbery, rubber, rabbit, rubbish, gibbous, ribbon, stubborn, chubby, crabby, flabby, hobby, lobby, bubbling, subblock, bubbly, bubble, dribble, pebble, rubble, scrabble, squabble, wobble, abbreviate*
>
> Final Position - *ebb*

However, on a few occasions the digraph *"bb"* is pronounced as two separate /b/, which is represented as /b.b/.

> *subbase, subbasement, subbranch, subbronchial*

Exceptionally, *"b"* can be silent in a certain number of words, usually before *"t"* and after *"m"*.

> *debt, doubt, subtle, aplomb, bomb, climb, comb, coulomb, crumb, dumb, jamb, lamb, limb, numb, plumb, succumb, thumb, tomb, womb, climber, plumber*

It is useful to know about the phonological process known as devoicing; in which a normally voiced consonant is replaced by a voiceless one when adjacent to unvoiced sounds. This common-ly happens when speaking fast. The words listed below could ex-hibit this phenomenon; with the voiced /b/ being devoiced to /p/.

> *club captain, crab salad, do not disturb sign, grab quick-ly, lab test, lobster, verb types*

Please, don't forget to record yourself saying the words, compare it to the model and make any necessary correc-tions. It is advisable to repeat this exercise on a daily basis. Furthermore, consider writing and practicing with tongue twisters and sentences that emphasize the pronunciation of /b/ in various topics and daily life scenarios.

Chapter 28

Minimal Pairs

p *and* b

T he primary distinction between the sounds /b/ and /p/ lies in the fact that /b/ is a voiced sound, while /p/ is produced solely with the release of air. Additionally, /b/ is articulated with less air released compared to /p/, making it a more challenging sound to differentiate at times due to the lack of easily discernible vocal cord vibration.

ca**p** - ca**b**	**p**air, **p**ear - **b**ear
cra**p** - cra**b**	**p**anned - **b**and, **b**anned
cu**p** - cu**b**	**p**are - **b**are
la**p** - la**b**	**p**at - **b**at
li**p** - li**b**	**p**atty - **b**atty
mo**p** - mo**b**	**p**ay - **b**ay
P, **p**ee - **B**, **b**e, **b**ee	**p**eak, **p**eek - **b**eak
pace - **b**ase	**p**eat - **b**eat, **b**eet

peed - bead

peep - beep

peer, pier - beer, bier

pelt - belt

per, purr - burr

perry - berry

pet - bet

pi, pie - bi, buy, by, bye

pig - big

pill - bill

pin - bin

pit - bit

pitch - bitch

plaid, played - blade

plank - blank

planned - bland

plaster - blaster

plays - blaze

plead - bleed

pleat - bleat

plot - blot

plume - bloom

plunder - blunder

plush - blush

poo - boo

pour - boar

praise, prays, preys - braise

prat - brat

prawn - brawn

preach - breech

pressed - breast

prick - brick

pride - bride

prig - brig

prim - brim

pull - bull

pup - pub

putt - but, butt

putter - butter

rip - rib

rope - robe

slap - slab

tap - tab

tripe - tribe

Chapter 29

Minimal Pairs

p *and* f

Both of these sounds are produced with just air and no voice. /p/ is plosive, similar to making a popping sound, and it cannot be prolonged once the mouth is open and the air is released. On the other hand, /f/ is a fricative sound that can be sustained for as long as you like by continuously blowing air through the gap between the articulators.

face - pace	fart - part
faced - paste	fashion - passion
fad - pad	fast - past
fail - pale	fat - pat
faint - paint	fate - pate
fair - pair	fax - packs
fan - pan	fear - pier
fang - pang	fee - P

feed - peed	flop - plop
feel - peel	flume - plume
feet - peat	flunk - plunk
felt - pelt	flush - plush
fen - pen	flux - plucks
fence - pence	fly - ply
fend - penned	foal - poll
ferry - perry	foes - pose
few - pew	fold - polled
fig - pig	folk - poke
file - pile	fond - pond
fill - pill	fool - pool
fin - pin	foot - put
finch - pinch	fop - pop
find - pined	ford - poured
fine - pine	fork - pork
firm - perm	found - pound
first - pursed	four - pour
fit - pit	fox - pox
fix - picks	frank - prank
flack - plaque	fray - pray
flan - plan	free - pre
flank - plank	fresher - pressure
fleas - please	fries - prize
fled - pled	frig - prig
flee - plea	fro - pro
fleet - pleat	from - prom
flight - plight	froze - prose

fry - pry

fug - pug

full - pull

fun - pun

fund - punned

funk - punk

fur - per

furl - pearl

fuss - pus

fade - paid

phase - pays

phrase - praise

Chapter 30

Minimal Pairs

b *and* v

The phonemes /b/ and /v/ are both produced with vibration of the vocal cords. The primary distinction is that /b/ is articulated with the contact of both lips, while /v/ is produced with the upper teeth touching the bottom lip. /v/ can be prolonged indefinitely, unlike /b/, which is a brief, explosive sound. Watch your mouth shape in the mirror to differentiate between them.

B - V		
bale - veil	berry - very	bolt - volt
ban - van	best - vest	bow - vow
bane - vein	bet - vet	bowels - vowels
bat - vat	bid - vid	bowl - vole
beer - veer	bile - vile	broom - vroom
bent - vent	biz - viz	bury - very
	boat - vote	curb - curve

dribble - drivel   gibbon - given   rebel - revel

dub - dove   jibe - jive   serb - serve

fiber - fiver   lobes - loaves   verb - verve

h

as in **how**

T his phoneme represents the consonant sound in words such as *"happy"*, *"history"* and *"who"*. /h/ lacks the place and manner of articulation of a prototypical consonant.

This sound is described as an unvoiced glottal fricative. You make it in the throat using the glottis. The vocal cords should be gently tightened to constrict the airway. Then, air is pushed up and released through the mouth only, creating a friction sensation in the vocal folds during the process. It is produced without vibrations of the vocal cords.

The term *"glottal"* only refers to the transitional state of the glottis; without any other structures like the tongue and alveolar ridge producing friction and turbulence. As a result, many phoneticians no longer classify /h/ as a fricative, but the term is commonly maintained for historical purposes.

The most common spelling for this sound is the letter *"h"*, which may appear in various positions within words.

Initial Position - *he, his, her, him, hers, himself, herself, have, has, had, how, here, habit, habitat, hair, hail, half, hall, hallelujah, hallucinate, ham, hamburger, hammer, hamster, hand, handle, handsome, handwritten, hang, hanger, haptic, happen, happy, harbor, hard, harm, harmony, harsh, harvest, hat, hate, hatred, hatch, head, heal, health, hear, heart, heat, heaven, heavy, hectic, heel, height, heist, helicopter, hell, hello, helmet, help, hemisphere, hence, hero, heroic, hesitate, hiatus, hide, high, hike, hill, hint, hippopotamus, hip, hire, history, hit, hives, hobby, hockey, hold, holy, holiday, hollow, home, honey, hook, hop, hope, horizon, horizontal, horn, horror, horse, hose, hospital, host, hostility, hot, hotel, house, hug, huge, hum, human, humid, hummingbird, hundred, hurricane, hurt, husbant, hydrogen, hypnotize, hypothesis, Haiti, Hannah, Hanukkah, Hawaii, Harold, Henry*

Middle Position - *adhesion, ahead, alcohol, anyhow, behave, behavior, behind, childhood, downhill, exhale, inhale, inherent, inhibit, lighthouse, mayhem, rehearse, reheat, unhappy, uphill, Oklahoma, Ohio, Yahoo*

By the same token, the digraph *"wh"* features the /h/ in the following words.

who, whom, whose, whoever, whole, wholesome, whore, anywho

Interestingly, a silent "h" can be encountered at the beginning, middle or end of words.

Initial Position - *heir, herb, honest, honor, hour*

Middle Position - *vehicle, vehement, exhaust, exhibit, exhilarate, exhort, exhume, ghost, ghastly, dinghy, piranha, rhyme, rhythm, shepherd, what, when, where, which, why, whether, white, Dachshund, Khalifa, marihuana*

Final Position - *Aliyah, Elijah, Hannah, hallelujah, Hanukkah, hurrah, ah, huh, oh, yeah*

On the other hand, English speakers often pronounce /h/ in words of Spanish origin as an approximation of the Spanish pronunciation.

jalapeno, junta, Juan, Jose, fajita, Xavier, Oaxaca

Please, don't forget to record yourself saying the words, compare it to the model and make any necessary corrections. It is advisable to repeat this exercise on a daily basis. Furthermore, consider writing and practicing with tongue twisters and sentences that emphasize the pronunciation of /h/ in various topics and daily life scenarios.

Chapter 32

Minimal Pairs
f *and* h

The phoneme /h/ is articulated with a release of air from a wide open mouth, maintaining the same mouth position as in words like "*h*at". It is comparable to blowing steam onto your glasses so you can clean them, and a bit like a sigh.

In contrast, the phoneme /f/ is produced with a more closed mouth, with the teeth close to or touching the bottom lip. Therefore, when saying words like "*f*at", it is necessary to open the mouth wider to articulate the vowel sound following /f/.

*f*aced - *h*aste	*f*all - *h*all	*f*at - *h*at
*f*ad - *h*ad	*f*ang - *h*ang	*f*ate - *h*ate
*f*ag - *h*ag	*f*are - *h*are	*f*ear - *h*ear
*f*ail - *h*ail	*f*arm - *h*arm	*f*ed - *h*ead
*f*air - *h*air	*f*art - *h*eart	*f*ee - *h*e

feed - he'd	fit - hit	force - horse
feel - he'll, heel	five - hive	found - hound
fees - he's	fizz - his	four - whore
feet - heat	foal - whole	fowl - howl
fell - hell	foam - home	fun - Hun
fence - hence	fob - hob	funky - hunky
few - hew	foe - hoe	funny - honey
fey - hay	foes - hose	furl - hurl
fight - height	fog - hog	phase - haze
fill - hill	fop - hop	phone - hone

as in *life*

T his phoneme represents the initial consonant sound in words such as *"light"* and *"loud"*, the middle one in *"blue"* and *"really"*, and the final one in *"meal"*, *"goal"* and *"ball"*.

This sound is described as a voiced alveolar lateral approximant. The tip or blade of the tongue rises up and presses against the alveolar ridge behind your teeth. You let the airflow escape around the sides of the tongue instead of the center and release it through the mouth without creating turbulence. Vibrate your vocal cords as you articulate it.

The /l/ can be pronounced in two different ways, depending on the presence of velarization and pharyngealization. The non-velarized form is named clear *"l"*, in which the back of the tongue stays down and the tip tends to be retracted to an alveolar position.

The clear "l" occurs before a vowel sound in a syllable, so it is usually found at the beginning of a word. It can also appear in the middle.

Initial Position - *lab, label, lack, lady, land, lane, large, last, late, launch, law, lay, lead, leader, leap, learn, lease, least, leather, leave, lecture, left, leg, legacy, legal, legend, length, lesbian, less, lesson, let, lethal, letter, level, liaison, license, lid, lie, life, lift, light, like, limit, line, link, lip, liquid, list, listen, little, live, load, local, log, long, look, loss, lost, lot, loud, love, low, lunch, lust*

Middle Position - *black, blame, bless, blind, blog, blond, blow, blue, problem, clash, claw, clay, clean, clear, clever, cliff, clip, clock, close, clover, club, clue, include, madly, sadly, flag, flash, flat, flavor, fleet, flesh, flex, flick, flip, floor, flow, flower, fluent, flush, flux, glad, gland, glass, gleam, glee, glimpse, glitch, glitter, globe, glove, glow, glue, glute, hyperbole, aimless, dimly, hamlet, harmless, warmly, cleanly, enlarge, mainly, online, only, sunlit, unless, unlike, place, plan, play, plea, plead, plenty, plot, plump, plural, plush, early, fairly, garlic, nearly, slam, slap, slay, sleep, slender, slight, slim, slip, slope, slow, slug, slump, butler, exactly, mostly*

This clear "l" can also be spelled as double "l" in the middle of the word.

actually, alley, allow, ally, ballad, ballet, challenge, fal-

low, gallery, gallon, malleable, really, shallow, swallow, valley, wallet, cellar, excellent, ellipse, fellow, intelligent, mellow, satellite, stellar, umbrella, billion, guillotine, illicit, miller, million, pillow, vanilla, village, villain, willow, collect, collage, college, collide, dollar, follow, hollow, holly, pollen, pollute, bullet, bulletin, lullaby, pullover

Alternatively, when /l/ occurs at the end of a syllable or before a consonant, the back of the tongue usually arches up a little toward the soft palate or the back of the throat; forming what is known as dark "l". This variant tends to be dental or denti-alveolar.

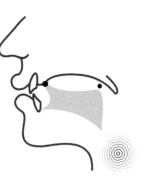

Middle Position - *albeit, album, albumin, elbow, bulb, bold, build, child, cold, field, fold, gold, guild, hold, mild, old, scold, shield, sold, told, weld, world, yield, fulfill, golf, self, selfish, shelf, wolf, algebra, algorithm, analgesic, bulge, indulge, nostalgia, vulgar, jailhouse, metalhead, wheelhouse, bulk, hulk, milk, silk, almost, Dalmatian, film, helm, overwhelm, realm, soulmate, ulnar, vulnerable, walnut, help, pulp, scalpel, sculp, whelp, already, alright, railroad, cavalry, jewelry, revelry, rivalry, also, balsam, else, false, impulse, Nelson, pulse, repulse, adult, alternative, assault, belt, bolt, built, catapult, cobalt, consult, cult, difficult, fault, guilt, halt, insult, melt, result, revolt, salt, vault, volt, elves, evolve, involve, resolve, shelves, silver, solve, twelve, valve, velvet, vulva*

Final Position - *actual, appeal, canal, coal, deal, dial, dual, equal, gal, goal, heal, manual, meal, mutual, pal, real, reveal, royal, seal, trial, usual, vial, bowel, compel, cruel, excel, feel, fuel, heel, hotel, peel, prequel, reel, steel, towel, wheel, bail, cocktail, fail, mail, nail, oil, rail, soil, spoil, tail, until, alcohol, cholesterol, control, cool, fool, patrol, pool, protocol, school, stool, tool, wool, foul, soul, curl, girl, pearl*

Magic "e" - *ale, dale, exhale, female, inhale, male, morale, pale, sale, scale, tale, whale, compile, exile, file, mile, pile, smile, style, tile, while, console, hole, parole, pole, role, stole, whole, capsule, lobule, module, molecule, mule, nodule, ridicule, rule, schedule, tubule, tule, argyle, gargoyle, style*

Moreover, the dark "l" can also be found at the ending and middle of a word spelled as "ll".

Final Position - *all, ball, call, fall, gall, hall, install, mall, shall, small, stall, wall, bell, cell, fell, hell, sell, shell, smell, spell, swell, tell, well, yell, bill, chill, drill, fill, fulfill, grill, hill, ill, instill, kill, skill, still, thrill, will, doll, poll, roll, scroll, stroll, toll, troll, bull, dull, full, pull, skull*

Middle Position - *billboard, pullback, fallback, hellcat, hillcrest, bulldog, bulldozer, hellfire, shellfish, skillful, tollgate, bullhorn, fulfillment, fullness, illness, wellness, bullpen, smallpox, wallpaper, ballroom, hillside, hilltop*

In the following examples, the letter "l" constitutes a syllabic consonant, wherein /l/ functions as an entire syllable. It replaces schwa within unstressed syllables after a consonant sound at the end of the word. Therefore, you can omit /ə/ and immediately go into the position for a dark "l".

Final Position - *global, herbal, tribal, verbal, modal, medal, pedal, sandal, scandal, suicidal, frugal, legal, animal, formal, minimal, normal, primal, anal, eternal, final, journal, original, personal, signal, terminal, principal, moral, mural, oral, several, spiral, viral, brutal, capital, fatal, metal, portal, postal, total, vital, lethal, approval, arrival, festival, naval, rival, local, vocal, critical, ethical, logical, magical, medical, musical, practical, physical, racial, social, special, label, rebel, model, channel, colonel, panel, tunnel, scalpel, cancel, pixel, pretzel, vessel, level, navel, novel, shovel, travel, pupil, council, fossil, pencil, tonsil, civil, devil, evil, symbol, idol, capitol, petrol, pistol, consul, awful, beautiful, careful, colorful, grateful, handful, helpful, joyful, painful, powerful, tasteful, useful, woeful, vinyl*

Magic "e" - *able, available, cable, double, liable, marble, noble, possible, stable, table, tremble, article, circle, cycle, miracle, particle, obstacle, uncle, vehicle, bundle, candle, fiddle, handle, idle, ladle, middle, paddle, baffle, riffle, shuffle, waffle, angle, eagle, giggle, jungle, single, tangle, ankle, sparkle, wrinkle, buckle, fickle, sickle, tackle, tickle, apple, couple, example, multiple, peo-*

ple, simple, battle, bottle, bustle, castle, gentle, hustle, little, mantle, subtle, title, turtle, whistle, dazzle, drizzle, embezzle, nozzle, puzzle, agile, docile, erectile, fertile, fragile, gentile, hostile, imbecile, missile, mobile, senile, servile, sterile, tactile, textile, versatile, volatile

Lastly, there is a certain number of words containing a silent "*l*".

could, should, would, solder, calf, half, behalf, calves, halves, salve, caulk, chalk, stalk, talk, walk, folk, yolk, folklore, balm, calm, palm, psalm, qualm, alms, almond, salmon, Lincoln

Please, don't forget to record yourself saying the words, compare it to the model and make any necessary corrections. It is advisable to repeat this exercise on a daily basis. Furthermore, consider writing and practicing with tongue twisters and sentences that emphasize the pronunciation of /l/ in various topics and daily life scenarios.

as in **r** _right_

T his phoneme represents the initial consonant sound in words such as "_r_iver" and "_wr_ong", and the final one in "fa_r_" and "ca_re_". The correct IPA phonetic symbol in narrow notation for /r/ is denoted as /ɹ/. In General American, the letter "r" is always pronounced.

It is described as a voiced postalveolar approximant. The tip of the tongue is raised and curled back behind the alveolar ridge, without making contact with the hard palate. You let the airflow escape around and over your tongue and release it through the mouth without creating turbulence. The vocal cords should vibrate during the articulation.

The /r/ sound is always spelled as "r" or "rr" and can appear in different positions within words.

Initial Position - *race, racial, radio, rage, rail, rain, raise, range, rank, rape, rare, rat, rate, rather, raw, ray, reach, read, ready, real, really, realize, realm, rear, reason, recent, receptor, record, recover, red, reduce, refer, reference, reform, refuse, regard, region, reign, relate, relative, release, relieve, rely, remain, remove, rent, report, require, rescue, research, resemble, resident, resist, resort, respect, respond, republic, rest, restore, result, retrieve, reveal, revenue, reverse, rice, rich, rid, ride, ridge, right, rim, ring, rise, risk, rival, river, road, rob, rock, rod, role, roll, roof, room, root, rose, rotate, rough, round, routine, route, row, royal, rude, rue, rule, run, rural, rush*

Middle Position - *brain, brave, bread, break, brief, brick, bright, bring, broad, brown, brush, brute, abrupt, algebra, embrace, eyebrow, vibrate, zebra, crab, crack, crash, cream, credit, crew, crime, crisis, critic, crop, cross, crow, cruise, crunch, crystal, acrobat, across, acrylic, concrete, describe, scratch, screen, script, drag, drain, drama, draw, dream, dress, drew, drink, drive, drop, drug, drum, android, bedroom, hydrant, scoundrel, syndrome, wondrous, frame, fraud, freak, free, fresh, fridge, friend, frog, from, front, frozen, fruit, fry, carefree, confront, defrost, refract, grain, grave, great, greed, green, grill, grip, gross, group, grow, degree, disgrace, hungry, integral, migrate, pedigree, vagrant, already, alright, railroad, cavalry, jewelry, rivalry, armrest, comrade, rimrock, genre, enroll, unreal, unrefined, unreliable, sun-*

ray, sunrise, practice, praise, prank, pray, press, prey, price, prime, prison, prize, profit, promise, prune, approve, comprise, empress, interpret, supreme, upright, classroom, crossroad, disregard, disrespect, disrupt, misread, sriracha, track, trade, train, trash, tread, treat, tree, trial, trim, trip, true, trust, truth, actress, control, hatred, matrix, neutral, ostrich, stretch, strove, threat, three, thrice, thrifty, thrill, thrive, throat, throne, through, throw, thrust, anthrax, urethra, every, several

On the other hand, /r/ has several limitations about what vowel sounds it can succeed. Those followed by /r/ are known as the American R-colored vowel sounds, as they are blended together with the phoneme /r/.

/ər/ - arise, around, barrage, garage, parade, variety, berserk, perceive, permit, thermometer, correct, forget, gorila, horizon, oregano, original, camera, different, entertain, hyperactive, intermediate, interview, lingerie, reverend, admirable, factory, ignorant, information, century, cultural, gestural, natural, angular, cellular, dollar, grammar, mortar, particular, popular, regular, similar, sugar, afterward, lizard, mustard, after, barber, beaver, better, center, consider, eager, father, gather, leader, leather, master, matter, member, meter, mother, neither, number, offer, order, over, rather, remember, sister, sober, teacher, theater, trigger, under, water, weather, whether, winter, amateur, soldier, actor,

author, behavior, color, director, doctor, editor, error, honor, horror, humor, investor, labor, liquor, major, motor, professor, sector, senior, terror, tutor, victor, pressure, scissure, closure, leisure, measure, seizure, azure, culture, future, nature, vulture, procedure, conjure, martyr. In this scenario, /r/ can also serve as a syllabic consonant, which replaces schwa within the same syllable. Therefore, you can omit /ə/ and go directly into the position for /r/.

/ɜːr/ - bird, first, girl, shirt, third, circle, circumstance, dirty, virgin, affirm, confirm, stirring, her, herb, merch, nerve, serve, verb, were, certain, mercy, nervous, perfect, service, verdict, alternative, emergency, external, concern, defer, err, earth, early, earn, heard, learn, search, burn, church, hurt, purse, turn, burden, curfew, hurry, murder, purchase, surgeon, turkey, urgent, concur, return, purr, word, world, work, worse, worth, worm, worry, journey, adjourn, courage, courtesy, connoisseur, entrepreneur

/ɔːr/ - or, for, nor, bor, chord, cord, fork, horn, lord, morse, north, pork, sort, torch, thorn, chorus, formal, fortune, glory, hormone, morning, normal, order, organic, portal, portrait, tornado, absorb, afford, conform, divorce, import, metaphor, passport, perform, record, support, unicorn, uniform, bore, core, chore, fore, core, lore, more, pore, score, snore, shore, sore, store, yore, wore, door, floor, boar, board, roar, soar, coarse, your,

156

four, pour, court, course, source, war, ward, warm, warn, quarter, aura, aurora, oracle, orange, orator, origami, origin, orrery, choreography, correspond, corridor, foreign, forest, horror, moral, torrid, authority, historical, majority, minority, priority, warrant, warranty, warrior, quarantine, quarrel

/ɑːr/ - *are, arm, art, bar, car, charge, dark, far, guard, hard, large, mark, park, scar, star, yard, archer, argument, artery, barber, bargain, cardigan, carpet, darling, garden, garlic, harbor, karma, larder, marble, narcissist, particle, party, sarcasm, target, antarctic, department, hierarchy, mascara, scenario, alarm, apart, bizarre, boulevard, depart, discard, guitar, radar, regard, remark, retard, heart, hearty, hearth, clerk, sergeant, borrow, sorrow, sorry, tomorrow*

/ɛr/ - *very, berry, cherry, ferry, merry, error, terror, errand, ceremony, cherish, derogate, heroism, stereo, terrace, terrible, territory, American, atmospheric, experiment, interrogate, area, vary, various, wary, Mary, scary, parent, garsh, hilarious, libertarian, proletarian, aquarium, bare, care, dare, fare, rare, scare, share, ware, declare, air, affair, chair, fair, hair, pair, stair, repair, millionaire, bear, wear, swear, tear, heir, their, there, where, werewolf, brassiere, compere, mayor, prayer, aerial, aeronaut, aerobics*

/ɪr/ - *miracle, mirror, spirit, nadir, souvenir, hero, zero,* cereal, series, period, experience, interior, bacteria, material, here, mere, sphere, austere, interfere, severe, beer, cheer, deer, peer, steer, career, engineer, reindeer, clear, dear, drear, ear, fear, gear, hear, near, tear, year, beard, appear, weird, weir, pier, tier, fierce, pierce, cashier, cavalier, chandelier, direct, direction, directive, director, directory, dirigible, giraffe, miraculous, mirage, Nirvana, berate, bereave, derange, derisive, derision, derivative, derive, prerelease, prerinse, prerogative, reradiate, reread, rerecord

/ʊr/ - plural, rural, crural, jury, sure, ensure, surety, lure, mature, pleura, pleurisy, poor, moor, boorish, tour, tourist, detour, lour, velour, amour, gourd, gourmet, bourbon, bourdon, bourgeois, courier, entourage

/jʊr/ - urine, Uranus, Uruguay, euro, Europe, bureau, bureaucrat, pure, impure, puritan, spurious, puerile, cure, secure, manicure, obscure, curable, curious, security, fury, furious, demure, mural

/ʊr/ or /jʊr/ - endure, manure, couture, durable, duration, during, neuron, neural, neurosis, aneurysm

/ær/ - arid, arrow, barrer, carry, carriage, characteristic, character, charity, guarantee, larynx, maritime, marry, marriage, narrative, narrow, parachute, paraglide, paragon, parallel, parent, parish, sparrow, apparent, comparison, embarrass

/aɪr/ - *direct, direction, directive, director, directory, irate, iris, irony, ironic, pirate, siren, spiral, viral, virus,* environment, inquiry, iron, choir, acquire, admire, as-pire, bonfire, conspire, crossfire, desire, empire, en-tire, esquire, expire, fire, hire, inspire, inquire, mire, re-tire, require, sapphire, satire, sire, shire, tire, umpire, vampire, wire, wildfire, Ireland

/aʊr/ - *our, hour, sour, four, dour, devour, cornflour*

In addition, the digraphs *"rh"* and *"wr"* are pronounced /r/ in the examples listed below.

rhythm, rhyme, wrack, wrap, wrapper, wrath, wreak, wreath, wreck, wreckage, wren, wrench, wrestling, wretched, wriggle, wring, wrinkle, wrist, write, wrong, wrote, playwright

However, there is a word where /r/ is not spelled *"r"*.

colonel /ˈkɜːrnəl/

Whereas the letter *"r"* is silent in the following word. This is the most common pronunciation in American English. However, the less common /ˈfɛbruːəriː/ is considered by many as the more traditional standard.

February

The following word also presents a silent "r".

Worcester

Last but not least, the position of the /r/ sound is different from the spelling in the next example.

comfortable /ˈkʌmftərbəl/

Please, don't forget to record yourself saying the words, compare it to the model and make any necessary corrections. It is advisable to repeat this exercise on a daily basis. Furthermore, consider writing and practicing with tongue twisters and sentences that emphasize the pronunciation of /r/ in various topics and daily life scenarios.

Chapter 35

Minimal Pairs

l and r

The phoneme /l/ involves a large flap of the tongue. To ensure you're not pronouncing /r/, bend your tongue as far back as you can in your mouth and flick it forward as you articulate /l/. The most effective method for making the distinction is to aim for minimal movement of the tongue when producing the /r/ sound.

alive - arrive	clash - crash
belly - berry	clown - crown
blacken - bracken	collect - correct
blew - brew	flea, flee - free
blight - bright	fleas - freeze
blue - brew	fly - fry
blues - bruise	glamor - grammar
blush - brush	gland - grand

glass - grass
glow - grow
jelly - jerry
lace - race
lack - rack
lag - rag
laid - raid
lair - rare
lake - rake
lamb - ram
lamp - ramp
lane - rain
lank - rank
lap - wrap
lash - rash
late - rate
lather - rather
law - raw
lay - ray
laze - raise
lead - read
lead, led - read, red
leader - reader
leap - reap
leech - reach
leer - rear
lentil - rental
lib - rib

lice - rice
lick - rick
lid - rid
lied - ride
lies - rise
light - right, rite, write
lighter - writer
limb - rim
lime - rhyme
lip - rip
list - wrist
lit - writ
load - road
loam - roam
loaves - roves
lob - rob
lock - rock
locker - rocker
locket - rocket
long - wrong
loom - room
loot - root
lope - rope
lot - rot
lout - rout
lows - rose
loyal - royal
lubber - rubber

luck - ruck lush - rush play - pray

lug - rug lust - rust splat - sprat

lump - rump lute - route splint - sprint

lung - rung pilot - pirate

m
as in ***more***

This phoneme represents the initial consonant sound in words such as *"man"* and *"milk"*, the middle one in *"image"* and *"grammar"*, and the final one in *"swim"* and *"game"*.

This sound is described as a voiced bilabial nasal. You close your lips and block the airflow in the vocal tract. Then, push air through the nasal cavity and let it escape exclusively through the nose. Vibrate your vocal cords during the articulation.

The letter *"m"* reliably produces this sound, and it can be observed in all different positions within a word.

Initial Position - *machine, make, man, manager, many, market, material, may, me, mean, medical, meet, mellow, member, merge, metal, method, middle, migrate,* military, milk, mind, minute, misery, miss, moment, money, more, mortgage, most, mother, motion, move, much, muffin, multiple, murder, museum, music, must, mutual, my, myc, mystery, mystical, myth, smack, small, smart, smash, smear, smell, smile, smirk, smite, smith, smog, smoke, smolder, smooth, smother, smudge, smug, smuggle

Middle Position - animal, human, image, woman, cement, comedy, moment, omelet, admit, family, permit, almost, demon, memory, academy, army, economy, enemy, amber, ambition, ambulance, combat, combine, combo, cucumber, embarrass, embassy, ember, gambit, hamburger, incumbence, member, number, symbol, zombie, campus, champagne, champion, company, compass, compile, computer, empathy, empower, example, important, impose, impulse, shampoo, stampede, sympathy, vampire, armchair, circumcise, circumference, comfort, hamlet, harmless, seamless, amnesia, chimney, gymnasium, insomnia, omnibus, comrade, circumstance, clumsy, crimson, drumstick, hamster, whimsical, something, warmth

Final Position - beam, cam, cream, dam, dream, exam, foam, gleam, ham, jam, program, roam, scam, scream, slam, steam, stream, team, deem, esteem, poem, redeem, seem, them, acclaim, aim, claim, dim, him, proclaim, rim, slim, swim, trim, bloom, boom, broom, doom, from, gloom, groom, mom, room, whom, zoom, cum, drum, helium, medium, museum, plum, podium, premium, sum, realm, overwhelm, film, alarm, arm, charm, farm, harm, warm, germ, term, confirm, firm, conform, form, inform, perform, platform, storm, uniform, worm

Magic "e" - blame, came, fame, flame, frame, game, name, same, shame, tame, extreme, meme, phoneme, scheme, supreme, theme, crime, lime, prime, regime, slime, sublime, time, chrome, come, dome, genome, gnome, home, some, syndrome, assume, consume, costume, exhume, fume, perfume, presume, resume, volume, enzyme, rhyme, thyme

In the following examples, the letter "m" constitutes a syllabic consonant, wherein /m/ functions as an entire syllable. It replaces schwa within unstressed syllables after a consonant sound at the end of the word. Consequently, you can omit /ə/ and immediately go into the position for /m/.

madam, problem, system, tandem, theorem, totem, victim, atom, blossom, bosom, bottom, custom, random, ransom, seldom, wisdom, album, forum, maximum

Magic "e" - welcome

Same occurs in the words below with an unwritten schwa before the syllabic "m".

pris(ə)m, alcoholis(ə)m, capitalis(ə)m, mechanis(ə)m,

166

> *organis(ə)m, racis(ə)m, touris(ə)m, algorith(ə)m, loga-*
> *rith(ə)m, rhyth(ə)m*

In addition, there are multiple words featuring the digraph *"mm"* pronounced as /m/.

> Middle Position - *comma, command, dilemma, gamma, grammar, mammal, summary, commend, comment, commercial, drummer, hammer, immense, immerse, recommend, summer, symmetry, commissary, commission, commit, committee, hummingbird, imminent, summit, swimming, commodity, common, hammock, immolate, summon, ammunition, communicate, community, hummus, dummy, mummy, tummy, yummy*

> Magic *"e"* - *femme, programme*

By the same token, the prefix *"in-"* becomes *"im-"* before *"m"*, however, only one /m/ is said.

> *immaculate, immaterial, immature, immeasurable, immediate, immemorial, immigrant, immobile, immoderate, immoral, immortal, immune, immutable*

Alternatively, you can oddly come across some words containing an *"mm"* pronounced as two separate /m/, represented as /m.m/.

> *roommate, teammate, homemade, homemaker*

Furthermore, the letter *"m"* can be accompanied by a silent letter.

> *aplomb, bomb, climb, comb, coulomb, crumb, dumb, jamb, lamb, limb, numb, plumb, succumb, thumb, tomb, womb, climber, plumber, autumn, column, condemn, damn, hymn, solemn, diaphragm, paradigm, phlegm, syntagm, balm, calm, palm, psalm, qualm, alms, almond, salmon*

And it can be silent in the following word.

> *mnemonic*

Lastly, as a result of the phonetic process known as assimilation, in which a consonant changes to be more similar to other nearby sound, /m/ before /f/ or /v/ may be neutralized and pronounced /ɱ/, a labiodental nasal.

> /ɱf/ - *circumference, circumflex, comfort, comfortable, harmful*

> /ɱv/ - *circumvent*

Please, don't forget to record yourself saying the words, compare it to the model and make any necessary corrections. It is advisable to repeat this exercise on a daily basis. Furthermore, consider writing and practicing with tongue twisters and sentences that emphasize the pronunciation of /m/ in various topics and daily life scenarios.

n

as in **new**

This phoneme represents the initial consonant sound in words such as *"nose"* and *"nice"*, the middle one in *"money"* and *"tennis"*, and the final one in *"clean"* and *"plane"*.

This sound is described as a voiced alveolar nasal. The tip and sides of the tongue touch the alveolar ridge and the airflow is blocked in the vocal tract. You redirect the blocked airflow through the nose only; don't let any air leave through the mouth. The vocal cords should vibrate during the articulation.

The letter *"n"* reliably evokes this sound in all different positions within a word.

Initial Position - *nail, name, nap, napkin, narrow, nation, native, natural, naughty, near, neck, need, neighbor, never, new, next, nice, niece, night, nine, noise, normal, north,* note, notice, nothing, now, nuclear, nude, null, number, nun, nurse, nut, snack, snail, snake, snap, snare, sneak, sneeze, sniff, snip, sniper, snippet, snitch, snob, snooze, snore, snot, snow, snub, snuck, snuffle, snug, snuggle

Middle Position - enable, enact, tuna, attorney, enemy, energy, honest, money, finish, punish, enough, honor, canyon, felony, many, bonbon, cranberry, rainbow, cancel, chance, dance, once, ounce, branch, inch, lunch, trench, candy, end, hand, kind, land, random, stand, under, bonfire, confetti, confirm, confront, angel, change, strange, moonlit, only, unless, environment, genre, sunrise, unravel, unreal, lense, sense, tense, consider, consist, consul, insect, inside, insist, insult, onset, ransom, gunshot, sunshine, contest, country, intend, interest, into, rent, want, anthem, canvas, envy, invade, invest, involve, enzyme, frenzy, conclusion, encourage, include, income, increase, pancake, melancholy, inquire, congratulate, engage, engrave, ingredient

Final Position - ban, bean, can, clean, fan, groan, lean, loan, man, mean, ocean, pan, plan, scan, tan, than, van, alien, green, keen, men, often, open, oven, pen, queen, ten, then, when, again, begin, bin, chain, coin, gain, gin, join, kin, main, pain, pin, plain, rain, ruin, sin, skin, stain, tin, train, twin, thin, vein, win, within, con, icon, iron, lion, moon, on, salon, son, soon, ton, upon, won, bun, down, fun, gun, nun, own, run, spun, sun, adorn, born, burn, concer**n**, cor**n**, ear**n**, gover**n**, hor**n**, lear**n**, moder**n**, mour**n**, patter**n**, por**n**, tur**n**, thor**n**, unicor**n**, war**n**, wester**n**, year**n**

Magic "e" - ca**ne**, cellopha**ne**, cra**ne**, huma**ne**, hurrica**ne**, la**ne**, pla**ne**, sa**ne**, ge**ne**, hygie**ne**, interve**ne**, obsce**ne**, sce**ne**, sere**ne**, combi**ne**, decli**ne**, defi**ne**, divi**ne**, fi**ne**, li**ne**, machi**ne**, mi**ne**, ni**ne**, pi**ne**, routi**ne**, shi**ne**, shri**ne**, swi**ne**, vacci**ne**, vi**ne**, wi**ne**, alo**ne**, bo**ne**, clo**ne**, condo**ne**, co**ne**, do**ne**, dro**ne**, go**ne**, lo**ne**, milesto**ne**, no**ne**, o**ne**, ozo**ne**, pho**ne**, postpo**ne**, pro**ne**, silico**ne**, sto**ne**, to**ne**, thro**ne**, zo**ne**, du**ne**, immu**ne**, pru**ne**, ru**ne**, tribu**ne**, tu**ne**

In the following examples, the letter "n" constitutes a syllabic consonant, wherein /n/ functions as an entire syllable. It replaces schwa within unstressed syllables after a consonant sound at the end of the word. Consequently, you can omit /ə/ and immediately go into the position for /n/.

hum**an**, org**an**, slog**an**, urb**an**, veter**an**, wom**an**, cert**ain**, mount**ain**, burd**en**, doz**en**, elev**en**, ev**en**, gard**en**, gold**en**, happ**en**, heav**en**, sev**en**, orig**in**, viol**in**, ars**on**, bac**on**, lem**on**, pard**on**, pers**on**, reas**on**, ribb**on**, wag**on**

Magic "e" - eng**ine**, exam**ine**, imag**ine**, fort**une**

In addition, there are multiple words displaying the digraph "nn" said as /n/.

Middle Position - ca**nn**abis, ci**nn**amon, i**nn**ate, mayo**n**-

naise, savanna, annex, banner, channel, connect, dinner, flannel, funnel, inner, kennel, manner, personnel, tunnel, winner, anniversary, bannister, cannibal, millennial, tennis, running, annotate, announce, annoy, cannon, cannot, innocent, innovation, annual, bunny, funny, Johnny, penny, skinny, sunny, tyranny, whinny

Final Position - inn

Magic "e" - cayenne, tonne

Conversely, you can oddly come across some words containing an "nn" pronounced as two separate /n/, represented as /n.n/.

meanness, unknown, unnatural, unnecessary

Furthermore, the letter "n" is sometimes accompanied by a silent letter.

knack, knead, knee, kneel, knew, knickers, knife, knight, knitting, knob, knock, knot, know, knowledge, knuckle, gnarl, gnarly, gnaw, gnome, gnu, align, sign, assign, consign, design, resign, benign, malign, campaign, champagne, deign, feign, foreign, reign, sovereign, cologne, poignant, pneumonia, handsome, sandwich, Wednesday, piranha, Lincoln

However, the following words feature a silent "n".

autumn, column, condemn, damn, hymn, solemn

As a result of the phonetic process known as assimilation, in which a consonant changes to be more similar to other nearby sound, /n/ before /p/ or /b/ may be pronounced /m/; leading to the creation of sequences such as /mp/ or /mb/. This phenomenon can be seen in the words listed below.

/mp/ - i**np**atient, i**np**ut, ma**np**ower, scree**np**lay, tur**np**ike, u**np**ack, u**np**aid, u**np**leasant, u**np**lug, u**np**opular, u**np**roven, u**np**unished

/mb/ - bo**nb**on, canno**nb**all, cra**nb**erry, o**nb**oard, rai**nb**ow, su**nb**athe, su**nb**urn, u**nb**alance, u**nb**earable, u**nb**lock, u**nb**roken, u**nb**orn

You may also encounter this pattern across word boundaries.

/mp/ - fu**n p**art, gree**n p**lanet, i**n p**eace, i**n p**lace, i**n p**osition, i**n p**rison, i**n p**ublic, lemo**n p**ie, mai**n p**urpose, mea**n p**eople, o**n p**ause, o**n p**oint, thi**n p**aper

/mb/ - eve**n b**attle, huma**n b**lood, i**n b**ed, i**n b**lue, multigrai**n b**read, ope**n b**ar, ope**n b**ook

Nevertheless, in most dictionaries the following words are shown with /np/ or /nb/.

/np/ - gu**np**owder, i**np**atient, i**np**ut, u**np**ack, u**np**leasant, u**np**opular

/nb/ - bo**nb**on, cra**nb**erry, rai**nb**ow, su**nb**athe, u**nb**earable, u**nb**elievable

Assimilation can also be observed when /n/ appears before /f/ or /v/, resulting in neutralization and pronunciation as /ɱ/, a labiodental nasal.

> /ɱf/ - *conference, confirm, conflict, conform, confront, confuse, enforce, infamous, infant, infect, infer, infinite, inform, informal*

> /ɱv/ - *canvas, convert, convey, convince, convoy, envelope, environment, invade, invasion, invent, inventory, inverse, invest, invisible, invite, invoke, invoice*

In a similar fashion, word boundaries can be identified as another location for /ɱf/.

> *clean fun, in family, in front, modern family, on film, on fire*

Please, don't forget to record yourself saying the words, compare it to the model and make any necessary corrections. It is advisable to repeat this exercise on a daily basis. Furthermore, consider writing and practicing with tongue twisters and sentences that emphasize the pronunciation of /n/ in various topics and daily life scenarios.

Chapter 38

Minimal Pairs

m *and* n

B oth sounds are made by the flow of air through your nose. The /m/ is formed by closing your lips, whereas for /n/, the lips remain open and the tip of your tongue touches the roof of your mouth behind your teeth to block the airflow.

am - an	dim - din
beam - bean	dime - dine
beam - been	dumb - dun
blame - blain	fame - feign
boom - boon	foam - phone
cam - can	game - gain
came - cane	gleam - glean
clam - clan	gnome - known
comb - cone	gram - gran
deem - dean	grim - grin

gum - gun

home - hone

mam - man

meme - mean

same - sane

scam - scan

seam, seem - scene, seen

sim - sin

skim - skin

spam - span

sperm - spurn

sum - son, sun

team, teem - teen

term - tern, turn

thyme, time - tine

tomb - 'toon

tome - tone

trams- - trans-

ŋ

as in

song

This phoneme represents the final consonant sound in words such as *"long"*, *"sing"* and *"thing"* and, of course, *"-ing"* forms. It is often referred to as *"agma"*, derived from the Greek word meaning *"fragment"*.

This sound is described as a voiced velar nasal. The back of the tongue contacts the soft palate and blocks the airflow in the vocal tract. Then you redirect the blocked air through the nose exclusively; don't let any air leave through your mouth. The vocal cords should vibrate as you make this sound.

/ŋ/ is commonly spelled as *"ng"* at the end of words, however it can also appear in the middle when a suffix is added.

Final Position - ba**ng**, boomera**ng**, ga**ng**, ha**ng**, musta**ng**, ra**ng**, sa**ng**, sla**ng**, twa**ng**, wa**ng**, accordi**ng**, bi**ng**, bri**ng**, cling, cunning, darling, during, earring, evening, fling, king, ling, lightning, meaning, middling, morning, notwithstanding, ping, offspring, pudding, ring, sibling, sing, sling, spring, Sterling, sting, string, swing, thing, willing, wing, wring, bubbling, coming, dancing, flowing, glowing, hiking, joking, kicking, liking, making, noting, pacing, roaming, staying, taking, updating, yelling, zipping, along, belong, long, prolong, song, strong, thong, tong, wrong, among, dung, lung, sung, diphthong, young

Magic "e" - meringue, tongue

Middle Position - hangover, banger, hanger, gangster, banging, hanging, slanging, dinghy, hummingbird, bringer, singer, stinger, stringer, clingy, accordingly, willingly, willingness, bringing, clinging, ringing, singing, springing, stinging, stringing, swinging, wringing, strongly, wrongly, belonging, longing, prolonging, amongst, angst, length, strength

Due to the phonetic process known as assimilation, in which a consonant changes to be more similar to other nearby sound, the letter "n" followed by "g" often forms the sound /ŋg/, which can be seen in the words listed below.

anger, angle, angler, angry, anguish, ganglion, kangaroo, language, languid, languish, mango, strangle, tangle, tango, triangle, wangle, penguin, bingo, English,

> *dingle, finger, jingle, jungle, linger, mingle, single, shingle, distinguish, extinguish, flamingo, lingual, linguistic, singular, Congo, congress, congruent, jongleur, bungle, fungus, hunger, hungry, jungle, mongrel*

By the same token, certain words have *"ng"* pronounced /ŋ/ in the root and /ŋg/ in their derivatives.

> *longer, longest, stronger, strongest, younger, youngest, prolongation, diphthongal, monophthongal*

You may also encounter this pattern across word boundaries.

> *even ground, fun game, Golden Globes, in grams, in gray, main gate, moon glow*

However, not all words containing *"ng"* have the /ŋ/ sound; in certain instances, it is pronounced /ng/ or /ndʒ/, which is known as lack of assimilation.

> /ng/ - *congratulate, engage, engrave, ingrained, ingredient, ungrateful*
>
> /ndʒ/ - *angel, danger, congest, contingency, dungeon, ginger, ingest, messenger, passenger, stranger, vengeance, engine, engineer, longitude, tangible, stingy, arrange, challenge, change, lounge, orange, strange*

Additionally, assimilation may also occur when *"n"* is succeeded by a /k/ sound, resulting in the phonetic sequence /ŋk/.

"nk" - a**nk**le, ba**nk**, ba**nk**rupt, bla**nk**, bla**nk**et, cra**nk**y, dra**nk**, fla**nk**, fra**nk**, ha**nk**, pla**nk**, pra**nk**, ra**nk**, sa**nk**, sta**nk**, ta**nk**, tha**nk**, bli**nk**, bri**nk**, dri**nk**, i**nk**, li**nk**, mi**nk**, pi**nk**, ri**nk**, shri**nk**, si**nk**, sli**nk**, spri**nk**le, sti**nk**, thi**nk**, twi**nk**le, wi**nk**, wri**nk**le, do**nk**ey, mo**nk**, bu**nk**, bu**nk**er, chu**nk**, chu**nk**y, du**nk**, ju**nk**, mo**nk**ey, pu**nk**, tru**nk**

"nc" - pa**nc**reas, sa**nc**tion, sa**nc**tify, sa**nc**timonious, sa**nc**tuary, sa**nc**tum, disti**nc**t, exti**nc**t, insti**nc**t, disti**nc**tion, zi**nc**, sy**nc**, co**nc**rete, adju**nc**t, pu**nc**tuate, pu**nc**ture, fu**nc**tion, ju**nc**tion, conju**nc**tion, u**nc**le

"nch" - a**nch**or, bro**nch**itis, sy**nch**ronization

"nq" - ba**nq**uet, co**nq**uest, i**nq**uest, reli**nq**uish, tra**nq**uility

"nx" as /ŋks/ - ji**nx**, ly**nx**, mi**nx**, lary**nx**, phary**nx**

"nx" as /ŋkʃ/ - a**nx**ious

Word boundaries can also be identified as another location for /ŋq/.

clea**n c**lothes, i**n c**ase, i**n c**ash, i**n c**omparison, i**n c**ontrast, o**n c**all

Nevertheless, in some particular words the *"n"* followed by /k/ lacks assimilation and is pronounced /nk/.

"nk" - ma**nk**ind, pai**nk**iller, u**nk**ind

"nc" - co**nc**lude, co**nc**lusion, e**nc**ourage, i**nc**lude, i**nc**ome, i**nc**orporate, i**nc**rease, pa**nc**ake, u**nc**lear

"nch" - mela**nch**olic, mela**nch**oly

"nq" - e**nq**uire, i**nq**uire, u**nq**uestionable

The digraph *"nx"* is pronounced /ŋz/ in the following word.

a**nx**iety

Furthermore, the /ŋk/ sound is formed in the word below, even though there is a silent *"d"* in the middle.

ha**ndk**erchief

The following homophones contain the sound /ŋ/: *ri**ng** - wri**ng***.

Please, don't forget to record yourself saying the words, compare it to the model and make any necessary corrections. It is advisable to repeat this exercise on a daily basis. Furthermore, consider writing and practicing with tongue twisters and sentences that emphasize the pronunciation of /ŋ/ in various topics and daily life scenarios.

Chapter 40

Minimal Pairs

n and ŋ

Both /n/ and /ŋ/ are articulated with the airflow directed through the nasal tract. While the sound for /n/ is produced by obstructing the airflow in your mouth using the front of the tongue, for /ŋ/ is using the back of the tongue.

ban - bang	hand - hanged
band, banned - banged	hun - hung
bun - bung	kin - king
chin - ching	pan - pang
clan - clang	pin - ping
din - ding	pond - ponged
don - dong	ran - rang
done, dun - dung	sin - sing
fan - fang	stun - stung
gone - gong	sun - sung

*tan - ta**ng***	*to**n** - to**ng**ue*
*thi**n** - thi**ng***	*wi**n** - wi**ng***
*ti**n** - ti**ng***	*wi**n**d - wi**ng**ed*

j

as in *year*

T his phoneme, also known as *"yod"*, represents the sound in words such as *"young"*, *"beyond"* and *"alien"*. It is similar to /iː/, but the tongue is closer to the teeth. There is an invisible /j/ in many words containing a *"u"* in their spelling.

It is described as a voiced palatal approximant. The middle and back part of the tongue is raised to the hard palate. You pull your tongue back and down slightly while pushing the air out of your mouth only, but not enough to produce a turbulent airstream. The vocal cords should vibrate in this sound.

Before other vowels, /j/ is normally spelled *"y"*. The following words demonstrate this statement.

Initial Position - **y**acht, **y**ak, **y**am, **y**ap, **y**ard, **y**arn, **y**awn,

> *yeah, year, yearn, yeast, yell, yelp, yes, yet, yew, yield, yip, yob, yoke, yolk, yore, York, you, young, your, youth, yowl, yo-yo, yarrow, yawning, yellow, Yemen, yesterday, yoga, yogurt, yummy, yuppie*
>
> Middle Position - *beyond, canyon, lawyer, sawyer, Kenya, Kanye*

There are some examples in which the *"y"* spelling does not sound as /j/. In most of the following words *"y"* has the /ɪ/ sound instead.

> *bayou, buyer, cayenne, coyote, kayak, papaya, crayon, layer, mayonnaise, payer, player, mayor, prayer, foyer, loyal, royal, voyage, voyager, flamboyant, destroyer, employer, employee*

In contrast, the letter *"i"* is pronounced /j/ in numerous words after the following sounds.

> /l/ - *brilliant, Italian, alien, million, billion, trillion, pavilion, rebellion, vermilion*
>
> /n/ - *California, Spaniard, Daniel, companion, dominion, minion, onion, opinion, union, reunion, senior, genius*
>
> /v/ - *fluvial, view, interview, preview, review, behavior, savior*
>
> /s/ - *concierge*

Curiously, the letter "*j*" is said /j/ in the two words listed below.

> *hallelujah, fjord*

The phonetic sequence /juː/ is very common in English and it has the special spellings "*u*", "*eu*", "*ew*", "*ue*" and "*ui*". When these spellings appear at the beginning of the words or are preceded by the labial and velar sounds /p/, /b/, /k/, /g/, /f/, /v/, /h/ and /m/, the "*yod*" is always pronounced /juː/.

> **u**se, **u**sual, **u**sually, **u**surp, **u**nion, **u**nit, **u**nited, **u**nicorn, **u**niform, **u**nique, **u**niverse, **u**niversity, **u**nanimous, **u**tensil, **u**terus, **u**tility, **u**tilize, **u**topia, **u**biquitous, **u**kulele, **U**ganda, **U**kraine, **eu**calyptus, **eu**logy, **eu**logize, **eu**phoria, **eu**thanasia
>
> /p/ - disp**u**te, p**u**ke, p**u**berty, p**u**bis, p**u**nitive, comp**u**ter, rep**u**tation, therap**eu**tic
>
> /b/ - ab**u**se, attrib**u**te, contrib**u**te, distrib**u**te, reb**u**ke, trib**u**ne, trib**u**te, deb**u**t, b**u**tane, alb**u**min, ib**u**profen, b**eau**t, b**eau**ty, b**eau**tiful. The word "*February*" has a silent "*r*" following the letter "*b*", therefore the "*u*" sounds as /juː/.
>
> /k/ - c**u**be, c**u**te, ac**u**te, acc**u**se, exc**u**se, electroc**u**te, exec**u**te, prosec**u**te, minusc**u**le, molec**u**le, C**u**ba, c**u**bic, c**u**bicle, c**u**cumber, c**u**min, C**u**pid, acc**u**mulate, evac**u**ate, evac**u**ation, occ**u**py, pec**u**liar, porc**u**pine, vac**u**um, innoc**u**ous, promisc**u**ous, c**u**e, barbec**u**e, resc**u**e, que**u**e

/g/ - *argument, jaguar, ambiguous, contiguous, argue*

/f/ - *fugue, fume, fuse, confuse, diffuse, infuse, pro-fuse, refuse, refuge, refute, perfume, fuel, fumigate, funeral, fuchsia, fuselage, fusion, futile, future, feud, feudal, few, curfew, nephew*

/v/ - *ovule, rivulet, revue*

/h/ - *huge, human, humid, humidity, humiliate, humility, humor, hue*

/m/ - *mule, mute, amuse, commute, immune, emu, mucus, municipality, museum, music, mutant, mutual, communicate, community, immunity, remunerate*

Interestingly, some examples with the sounds /l/, /n/ and /θ/ also fall into the previous group, even though they are not labial or velar sounds.

/l/ - *volume, voluminous, evaluate, evaluation, valuation, valuable, value*

/n/ - *minute, annual, genuine, manual, menu, January, manuscript, continuous, ingenuous, tenuous, continue, ingenue, venue, revenue*

/θ/ - *Matthew*

Furthermore, the word below is a special case of /juː/ with *"ou"* spelling.

> *bay**ou***

When the spellings *"u"*, *"eu"*, *"ew"*, *"ue"* and *"ui"* are preceded by the alveolar and dental sounds /t/, /d/, /s/, /z/, /θ/ and /n/, the *"yod"* is pronounced by some speakers, and not by others. In General American the yodless pronunciation is more frequent.

> /t/ - t**u**be, t**u**lle, t**u**ne, altit**u**de, aptit**u**de, attit**u**de, latit**u**de, longit**u**de, magnit**u**de, multit**u**de, solit**u**de, ast**u**te, destit**u**te, prostit**u**te, substit**u**te, cost**u**me, st**u**dent, st**u**pid, t**u**bular, t**u**na, t**u**tor, t**u**torial, t**u**ition, int**u**ition, constit**u**tion, fort**u**itous, grat**u**ity, instit**u**tion, longit**u**dinal, opport**u**nity, st**ew**, st**ew**ard, T**u**esday
>
> /d/ - d**u**de, d**u**ke, d**u**ne, ded**u**ce, introd**u**ce, prod**u**ce, red**u**ce, sed**u**ce, d**u**al, d**u**el, d**u**o, d**u**odenum, d**u**bious, d**u**ty, cond**u**it, d**eu**ce, d**ew**, d**u**e, resid**u**e
>
> /s/ - ass**u**me, caps**u**le, cons**u**me, s**u**icide, s**u**per, s**u**perficial, s**u**pervise, s**u**premacy, s**u**preme, s**u**shi, s**u**ture, ps**eu**do, ps**eu**donym, mass**eu**se, s**ew**er, s**ew**age, s**u**e, purs**u**e, ens**u**e, s**u**it, s**u**itable
>
> /z/ - pres**u**me, res**u**me, exh**u**me, ex**u**de, z**u**cchini, ex**u**berant
>
> /θ/ - enth**u**se, enth**u**siastic

/n/ - n**u**de, n**u**ke, n**u**ance, n**u**clear, n**u**cleus, n**u**meral, n**u**merous, N**u**tella, n**u**trient, n**u**trition, ne**u**tral, ne**u**ter, ne**u**tron, pne**u**matic, pne**u**monia, mane**u**ver, kn**ew**, n**ew**, aven**ue**, retin**ue**, reven**ue**, n**ui**sance

Similarly, the word below may be pronounced with either /uː/ or /juː/, despite being at the beginning of the word.

Uber

The sequence /jʊr/ is another configuration in which the *"yod"* is present. In the following words, the *"yod"* is always pronounced. This occurs when the spellings *"u"* and *"eu"* appear at the beginning of words or are preceded by the labial and velar sounds /p/, /b/, /k/, /f/ and /m/.

ureter, **u**rine, **U**ranus, **U**ruguay, **eu**ro, **Eu**rope, **Eu**ropean, di**u**retic

/p/ - p**u**re, imp**u**re, guip**u**re, purp**u**re, p**u**ritan, p**u**rity, p**u**rulent, sp**u**rious, p**u**erile

/b/ - b**u**reau, b**u**reaucracy, b**u**reaucrat

/k/ - c**u**re, manic**u**re, obsc**u**re, proc**u**re, sinec**u**re, sec**u**re, c**u**rable, c**u**rettage, c**u**rious, sec**u**rity

/f/ - f**u**ror, f**u**ry, f**u**rious

/m/ - dem**u**re, m**u**ral

On the other hand, there are some words in which some speakers pronounce *"yod"* in them as /jʊr/. Other speakers prefer the yodless /ʊr/. This occurs when the spellings *"u"* and *"eu"* are preceded by the alveolar sounds /d/, /t/ and /n/.

> *end**ur**e, man**ur**e, cout**ur**e, d**ur**able, d**ur**ation, d**ur**ing, n**eu**-ron, n**eu**ral, n**eu**rosis, an**eu**rysm*

In addition to all of this, you can find another sequence containing the *"yod"*. Undoubtedly, this is the /j/ followed by the most common phoneme of the English language, schwa /ə/. This sequence /jə/ can be visualized with the *"u"* spelling.

> /p/ - *stip**u**late, pop**u**lar, scap**u**lar, corp**u**lent, op**u**lent, dep**u**ty*
>
> /b/ - *amb**u**late, discombob**u**late, tab**u**late, lob**u**lar, tub**u**-lar, amb**u**lance, fab**u**lous, turb**u**lent, vocab**u**lary*
>
> /k/ - *acc**u**rate, artic**u**late, calc**u**late, immac**u**late, spec-**u**late, binoc**u**lars, circ**u**lar, molec**u**lar, musc**u**lar, par-tic**u**lar, sec**u**lar, spectac**u**lar, circ**u**lation, consec**u**tive, curric**u**lum, doc**u**ment, masc**u**line, Merc**u**ry, spec**u**lum, succ**u**lent*
>
> /g/ - *coag**u**late, inaug**u**rate, reg**u**late, inaug**u**ral, reg**u**lar, sing**u**lar, triang**u**lar, coag**u**lation, fig**u**re*
>
> /m/ - *acc**u**mulate, em**u**late, sim**u**late, stim**u**late, comm**u**-nist, form**u**la*

/n/ - *granulate, annular, granular, monument, manipulate*

/l/ - *cellular, soluble, failure*

Another spelling for /jə/ is the letter "*i*" or "*y*" followed by a vowel.

brilliant, Italian, alien, million, billion, trillion, pavilion, rebellion, vermilion, California, Spaniard, Kenya, Daniel, Kanye, canyon, companion, dominion, minion, onion, opinion, union, reunion, senior, genius, fluvial, behavior, savior

This also occurs in the next word, but in this case, the vowel follows the letter "*j*".

hallelujah

Moreover, the /jə/ is specially produced in "*a*" preceded by "*n*".

lasagna, poignant

And last but not least, the sound pattern /jæ/ also takes place in "*a*".

cognac, pinata

Please, don't forget to record yourself saying the words, compare it to the model and make any necessary corrections. It is advisable to repeat this exercise on a daily basis. Furthermore, consider writing and practicing with tongue twisters and sentences that emphasize the pronunciation of /j/ in various topics and daily life scenarios.

Chapter 42

W
as in warm

T his phoneme represents the sound in words such as "<u>w</u>all", "<u>w</u>ater" and "<u>w</u>orld". It is similar to the sound /uː/, but the lips are slightly more closed when producing /w/.

It is described as a voiced labio-velar approximant. You start by rounding your lips into a tight circle, and while doing this, you raise the back part of the tongue toward the soft palate. Your tongue should not touch any other structures of your mouth. Then, you widen your lips and spread them into the shape of the vowel following it as you move the tongue forward and push the air out of your mouth. You must vibrate your vocal cords as you make this sound.

The most common spelling for this phoneme is "w". It can be found in the following words.

Initial Position - *waffle, wagon, waist, wait, wake, walk, wall, wallet, wallpaper, walnut, walrus, wander, want, war, ware, warm, warn, warrant, was, wash, wasp, waste, watch, water, waterfall, waterproof, way, wave, we, web, weak, wear, weather, wedding, weed, week, weekend, weigh, well, welcome, were, wide, wife, wig, wild, will, win, wind, window, wing, wire, wisdom, wish, with, witch, wolf, woman, won, wonder, wonderful, wood, word, work, world, worm, worry, would, Walter, Washington*

Middle Position - *always, anyway, awake, award, aware, away, backward, between, cobweb, forward, framework, hardware, highway, homework, kiwi, likewise, mouth-wash, microwave, network, reward, sandwich, schwa, seaweed, sidewalk, software, swaddle, sweet, swift, swim, swing, switch, tweet, twice, twin, twist, twitch, worldwide, Delaware, Edward, Gwendolyn, Hawaii, Hollywood, Rwanda, Swede, Sweden, Swiss, Switzerland, Taiwan, Twitter*

In addition, the digraph *"wh"* is another representation.

whale, what, when, where, whence, which, why, whatever, whenever, wherever, whichever, wheel, whether, while, whisper, white, anywhere, everywhere, somewhere, somewhat, meanwhile

On the other hand, the letter *"u"* features this semivowel in a certain number of words in which *"u"* is preceded by *"g"* and *"q"*.

After "g" - guacamole, Guam, Guatemala, guava, iguana, jaguar, language, lingual, Managua, Nicaragua, Paraguay, Uruguay, anguish, distinguish, linguist, linguistic, penguin, sanguine, sanguineous

After "q" - quack, quaff, quake, qualify, quality, qualm, quandary, quantify, quantity, quark, quarrel, quarter, quash, queen, quell, quench, query, question, quick, quid, quill, quilt, quirk, quit, quiet, quite, quiver, quiz, quora, quota, quote, quotient, aqua, banquet, bequeath, consequence, eloquence, enquire, equal, equip, equipment, equivalent, frequent, inquest, inquire, liquid, marquess, request, require, sequel, sequin, soliloquy, squad, squalid, squander, square, squash, squat, squeak, squeeze, squid, squint, squire, squirm, squirt, turquoise, acquaint, acquaintance, acquiesce, acquire, acquit, Macquarie

In the same way, the "u" evokes /w/ when preceded by other letters in the words listed below, which are primarily loanwords from Spanish.

cuisine, suede, suite, persuade, chihuahua, marijuana, San Juan, Buenos Aires, Ecuador, Kuala Lumpur, Puerto Rico, Venezuela

Moreover, it is portrayed in the letters "o" and "ou".

choir, quinoa, **ou**ija, **Ou**agadougou

And some other words have an invisible /w/ in front of "o".

> **(w)one, (w)once**

There are a number of loanwords from French containing the phonetic sequence /wɑː/ in the letter combination "oi".

> v**oi**là, abatt**oir**, boud**oir**, dev**oir**, m**oir**e, mem**oir**e, pei-
> gn**oir**, repert**oir**e, reserv**oir**, vouss**oir**

Similarly, a few instances include a silent final "s".

> bourge**ois**, pat**ois**, trav**ois**

On the contrary, in the following words the letter "w" is pronounced as /ʊ/.

> bo**w**, blo**w**, ro**w**, blo**w**ing, ro**w**ing, o**w**n, gro**w**n, kno**w**n,
> ho**w**, bo**w**, vo**w**, bo**w**ing, vo**w**ing, po**w**er, flo**w**er, vo**w**el,
> to**w**el, do**w**n, to**w**n, cro**w**d, po**w**der

Ultimately, many words that have "w" in their spelling don't have /w/ in their pronunciation. You may find numerous examples with a silent "w" listed below.

> After /s/ - ans**w**er, s**w**ord

> Before /h/ - **w**ho, **w**hom, **w**hose, **w**hoever, **w**hole, **w**hole-
> some, **w**hore

Before /r/ - *wrack, wrangle, wrap, wrapper, wrath, wreak, wreath, wreck, wreckage, wren, wrench, wrestle, wrestling, wretched, wriggle, wring, wrinkle, wrist, wrong, wrote, wrought, playwright*

Greenwich

In a similar fashion, *"w"* sometimes accompanies other letters to create a different vowel sound.

awry, knowledge, law, draw, saw, drawing, dawn, crawl, lawyer, awful, awesome, awkward, two, blew, crew, chew, new, few, view, viewing

Please, don't forget to record yourself saying the words, compare it to the model and make any necessary corrections. It is advisable to repeat this exercise on a daily basis. Furthermore, consider writing and practicing with tongue twisters and sentences that emphasize the pronunciation of /w/ in various topics and daily life scenarios.

Chapter 43

Silent
consonant
Letters

I n linguistics, a silent letter refers to a letter that is included in the written form of a word but does not affect the pronunciation. In English, it is not uncommon to encounter digraphs or trigraphs where one or more letters are not pronounced, whether they are consonants or vowels.

Listed below you can find a number of words in which consonants act as silent letters.

"s" - i*s*land, i*s*le, ai*s*le, vi*s*count, debri*s*, chassi*s*, preci*s*, bourgeoi*s*, patoi*s*, travoi*s*, rendezvou*s*, *s*chwa, *s*chist, Arkansa*s*

"z" - laisse*z*-faire, rende*z*vous

"c" - as*c*ent, cres*c*ent, iras*c*ible, mis*c*ellaneous, nas*c*ent, rescind, scene, scepter, science, visceral, evanesce, reminisce, Bicester, Gloucester, Leicester, Worcester, indict, victual

"ch" - yacht

"th" - asthma, isthmus

"k" - knack, knead, knee, kneel, knew, knickers, knife, knight, knitting, knob, knock, knot, know, knowledge, knuckle

"g" - gnarl, gnarly, gnaw, gnome, gnu, align, sign, assign, consign, design, resign, benign, malign, arraign, campaign, champagne, deign, feign, reign, foreign, sovereign, coign, poignant, cologne, diaphragm, syntagm, paradigm, phlegm, cling, hang, sing, long, lung, coming, running, walking, willing, hanger, hangover, hanging, clingy, longing, singer, singing, willingly

"gh" - dough, though, although, borough, thorough, bough, plough, sough, drought, bought, brought, fought, thought, caught, naught, taught, daughter, through, brougham, straight, eight, neighbor, weigh, fight, high, knight, light, might, night, right, thigh, height, sleight

"t" - apostle, bristle, bustle, castle, gristle, hustle, nestle, pestle, rustle, thistle, whistle, wrestle, Mistletoe, chas-

ten, christen, fasten, glisten, hasten, listen, moisten, often, soften, chestnut, Christmas, mortgage, ballet, bouquet, buffet, cabaret, cachet, chalet, gourmet, ricochet, tourniquet, valet, depot, rapport, debut

"d" - handsome, handkerchief, sandwich, Wednesday

"p" - coup, receipt, cupboard, raspberry, corps, pneumonia, psalm, pseudo, pseudonym, psoriasis, psych, psychic, psychology, psychiatry, psychiatrist, psychotherapy, psychedelic, psychopath, psychotic

"b" - debt, doubt, subtle, aplomb, bomb, climb, comb, coulomb, crumb, dumb, jamb, lamb, limb, numb, plumb, succumb, thumb, tomb, womb, climber, plumber

"h" - heir, herb, honest, honor, hour, vehicle, vehement, exhaust, exhibit, exhilarate, exhort, exhume, ghost, ghastly, dinghy, piranha, rhyme, rhythm, shepherd, what, when, where, which, why, whether, white, Dachshund, Khalifa, marihuana, Aliyah, Hannah, hallelujah, Hanukkah, hurrah, ah, huh, oh, yeah

"l" - could, should, would, solder, calf, half, behalf, calves, halves, salve, caulk, chalk, stalk, talk, walk, folk, yolk, folklore, balm, calm, palm, psalm, qualm, alms, almond, salmon, Lincoln

"r" - February, Worcester

"m" - **m**nemonic

"n" - autum**n**, colum**n**, condem**n**, dam**n**, hym**n**, solem**n**

"w" - ans**w**er, s**w**ord, **w**ho, **w**hom, **w**hose, **w**hoever, **w**hole, **w**holesome, **w**hore, **w**rack, **w**rangle, **w**rap, **w**rapper, **w**rath, **w**reak, **w**reath, **w**reck, **w**reckage, **w**ren, **w**rench, **w**restle, **w**restling, **w**retched, **w**riggle, **w**ring, **w**rinkle, **w**rist, **w**rong, **w**rote, **w**rought, play**w**right, t**w**o, a**w**ry, la**w**, dra**w**, sa**w**, dra**w**ing, da**w**n, cra**w**l, la**w**yer, a**w**ful, a**w**e-some, Green**w**ich

"j" - mari**j**uana

"x" - Bordeau**x**, fau**x**, fau**x** pas, rou**x**, Siou**x**

Due to its widespread use in the English language, the magic "e" warrants its individual recognition. This phonetic marker indicates that the letter "e" at the end of a word doesn't produce a sound, but rather alters the pronunciation of the word. The technical term for *"magic e"* is *"split digraph"*, denoting that "e" is the second letter in a split digraph with another vowel sound. Its purpose is to signal that a short vowel sound should generally be shifted into a long vowel sound. This digraph is interrupted by a consonant letter in the middle.

massag**e**, mor**e**, lov**e**, alon**e**, brows**e**, choos**e**, los**e**, fenc**e**, rehears**e**, bridg**e**, fertil**e**, vintag**e**, breath**e**, her**e**, car**e**, sur**e**, mak**e**, nic**e**, choic**e**, opaqu**e**, physiqu**e**, leagu**e**, fatigu**e**, vagu**e**, rogu**e**

Support the author!

REVIEW THE BOOK ON AMAZON!

@VICGARBOOKS

Bibliography

Albert Sydney Hornby, and Diana Lea. Oxford Advanced Learner's Dictionary of Current English. Oxford University Press, 2020.

Allen, R E, et al. The Concise Oxford Dictionary of Current English. Oxford: Clarendon Press: Oxford University Press, 1990.

Brookes, Ian. The Chambers Dictionary. London, Chambers, 2014.

Giegerich, Heinz J. English Phonology : An Introduction. Cambridge, Cambridge University Press, 2006.

International Phonetic Association. Handbook of the International Phonetic Association : A Guide to the Use of the International Phonetic Alphabet. Cambridge, Cambridge University Press, 1999.

Marriam-Webster Dictionary. The Merriam-Webster Dictionary. Massachusetts Merriam-Webster, Inc, 2006.

Stevenson, Angus. Oxford Dictionary of English. 3rd ed., Oxford, Oxford University Press, 2010.

Index

T

turbulence 12, 26, 33, 40, 45, 53, 58, 64,
68, 142, 147, 153

U

unstressed syllable 151, 166, 171

V

velar sound 186, 187, 189

vibration 1, 26, 40, 53, 64, 77, 96, 127,
136, 140, 142

vocal cords 1, 12, 26, 33, 40, 45, 53, 58,
62, 64, 68, 75, 77, 86, 93, 96, 109,
120, 127, 132, 140, 142, 147, 153,
164, 169, 177, 184, 193

vowel sound 10, 14, 17, 18, 70, 90, 99,
102, 111, 114, 116, 145, 148, 155,
197, 201

Y

yod 184, 186, 189, 190

yodless 188, 190